First World War
and Army of Occupation
War Diary
France, Belgium and Germany

61 DIVISION
183 Infantry Brigade
Suffolk Regiment
11th Battalion
1 June 1918 - 15 November 1919

WO95/3062/2

The Naval & Military Press Ltd
www.nmarchive.com
Published in association with The National Archives

Published by

The Naval & Military Press Ltd

Unit 10 Ridgewood Industrial Park,

Uckfield, East Sussex,

TN22 5QE England

Tel: +44 (0) 1825 749494

www.naval-military-press.com

www.nmarchive.com

This diary has been reprinted in facsimile from the original. Any imperfections are inevitably reproduced and the quality may fall short of modern type and cartographic standards.

© **Crown Copyright**
Images reproduced by permission of The National Archives, London, England, 2015.

Contents

Document type	Place/Title	Date From	Date To
Heading	War Diary 11th (S) Bn The Suffolk June 1st-30th 19		
War Diary	Lalacque Camp	01/06/1918	02/06/1918
War Diary	Guarbecque	03/06/1918	09/06/1918
War Diary	St. Floris Sector H.Q (Sheet 36.A)	09/06/1918	17/06/1918
War Diary	Hamet Billet	18/06/1918	20/06/1918
War Diary	St Floris Sector (Sheet 36a)	21/06/1918	30/06/1918
Operation(al) Order(s)	11th Suffolks Operation Order No.33	08/06/1918	08/06/1918
Operation(al) Order(s)	11th Suffolks Operation Order No.35	12/06/1918	12/06/1918
Operation(al) Order(s)	11th Suffolks Operation Order No.36	16/06/1918	16/06/1918
Operation(al) Order(s)	11th Suffolks Operation Order No.38	20/06/1918	20/06/1918
Operation(al) Order(s)	11th Suffolks Operation Order No.39	24/06/1918	24/06/1918
Heading	War Diary 11th (S) Bn The Suffolk Regt (Camb) July 1st-31st 1918 Vol 31		
War Diary	Hamet Billet	01/07/1918	04/07/1918
War Diary	St. Floris Sector Left Sub Section	05/07/1918	09/07/1918
War Diary	St. Floris Sector	10/07/1918	10/07/1918
War Diary	St. Hilaire	11/07/1918	16/07/1918
War Diary	Linghem	17/07/1918	22/07/1918
War Diary	Campagne (Sheet 27)	23/07/1918	27/07/1918
War Diary	Campagne	28/07/1918	31/07/1918
Operation(al) Order(s)	11th Suffolks Order No.42	03/07/1917	03/07/1917
Miscellaneous	Programme of Work	12/07/1918	12/07/1918
Operation(al) Order(s)	11th Suffolks Order No.44	06/07/1918	06/07/1918
Operation(al) Order(s)	11th Suffolks Order No.45	10/07/1918	10/07/1918
Operation(al) Order(s)	11th Suffolks Order No.47	16/07/1918	16/07/1918
Miscellaneous	11th Battalion The Suffolk Regt Defence Instructions No.1	19/07/1918	19/07/1918
Miscellaneous	11th Battalion The Suffolk Regiment Defence Instructions No.2	19/07/1918	19/07/1918
Miscellaneous	11th (S) Bn The Suffolk Regiment Defence Instructions No.3		
Miscellaneous	Programme of Work	19/07/1918	19/07/1918
Heading	War Diary 11th Bn Suffolk Rgt (Camp) August 1st 31st 1918 Vol 32		
War Diary	Linghem	01/08/1918	06/08/1918
War Diary	La Lacque	07/08/1918	07/08/1918
War Diary	Le Sart Sector (Sheet 36A)	08/08/1918	09/08/1918
War Diary	Vallorba Camp	10/08/1918	14/08/1918
War Diary	Arrewage Sector (Sheet 36 A.N.E)	15/08/1918	31/08/1918
Miscellaneous	11th Battalion The Suffolk Regt Defence Instructions No.1	02/08/1918	02/08/1918
Miscellaneous	11th Battalion The Suffolk Regiment Defence Instructions No.2		
Miscellaneous	11th Bn The Suffolk Regt Defence Instructions No.3		
Operation(al) Order(s)	11th Suffolks Order No.32	01/06/1918	01/06/1918
Operation(al) Order(s)	11th Suffolks Operation Order No.34	03/06/1918	03/06/1918
Miscellaneous	Training Programme	03/08/1918	03/08/1918
Operation(al) Order(s)	11th Suffolks Order No.50	06/08/1918	06/08/1918
Operation(al) Order(s)	11th Suffolks Order No.51	09/08/1918	09/08/1918
Operation(al) Order(s)	11th Suffolks Order No.52	14/08/1918	14/08/1918

Operation(al) Order(s)	11th Suffolks Order No.53	18/08/1918	18/08/1918
Operation(al) Order(s)	11th Suffolks Order No.54	20/08/1918	20/08/1918
Operation(al) Order(s)	11th Suffolks Order No.55	21/08/1918	21/08/1918
Operation(al) Order(s)	11th Suffolks Order No.41	29/06/1918	29/06/1918
Operation(al) Order(s)	11th Suffolks Order No.43	06/07/1918	06/07/1918
Operation(al) Order(s)	11th Suffolks Operation Order No.37	19/06/1918	19/06/1918
Miscellaneous	Lorries are allotted as under		
Operation(al) Order(s)	11th Suffolks Order No.48	29/07/1918	29/07/1918
Operation(al) Order(s)	11th Suffolks Order No.56	25/08/1918	25/08/1918
Operation(al) Order(s)	11th Suffolks Order No.57	24/08/1918	24/08/1918
Operation(al) Order(s)	11th Suffolks Order No.58	24/08/1918	24/08/1918
Miscellaneous	Appendix "A"	24/07/1918	24/07/1918
Miscellaneous	11th Battalion The Suffolk Regt. Programme of Work	26/07/1918	26/07/1918
Miscellaneous	11th Battalion The Suffolk Regt Defence Instructions		
Operation(al) Order(s)	11th Suffolks Order No.49	31/07/1918	31/07/1918
Miscellaneous	Lorries are allotted as under		
Heading	War Diary 11th (S) Bn The Suffolk Regt (Camb) September 1st-30th 1918 Vol 33		
War Diary	Sheet 36A. N.E. Arrewage Sector	01/09/1918	01/09/1918
War Diary	Villorba Camp	02/09/1918	04/09/1918
War Diary	Rue Montigny	05/09/1918	05/09/1918
War Diary	Cobalt Cottages	06/09/1918	07/09/1918
War Diary	Sheet 36 N.W. G.23.a.84 G.18.a.15.15	08/09/1918	11/09/1918
War Diary	L.28.b.9.9	12/09/1918	20/09/1918
War Diary	G.20.b.4.8	21/09/1918	28/09/1918
War Diary	L.28.b.9.9	29/09/1918	30/09/1918
Operation(al) Order(s)	11th Suffolks Order No.58	31/08/1918	31/08/1918
Operation(al) Order(s)	11th Suffolks Order No.59	04/09/1918	04/09/1918
Operation(al) Order(s)	11th Suffolks Order No.60	05/09/1918	05/09/1918
Operation(al) Order(s)	11th Suffolks Order No.61	07/09/1918	07/09/1918
Operation(al) Order(s)	11th Suffolks Order No.62	11/09/1918	11/09/1918
Operation(al) Order(s)	11th Suffolks Order No.63	21/09/1918	21/09/1918
Operation(al) Order(s)	Extract from Bde Order No. 248	24/09/1918	24/09/1918
Operation(al) Order(s)	11th Suffolks Order No.64	24/09/1918	24/09/1918
Operation(al) Order(s)	11th Battalion The Suffolk Regiment Order No.65	26/09/1918	26/09/1918
Operation(al) Order(s)	11th Suffolks Order No.66	28/09/1918	28/09/1918
Miscellaneous	Defence Instructions Nau Monde Section	28/09/1918	28/09/1918
Miscellaneous			
Heading	War Diary 11th (S) Bn The Suffolk Regt (Cambs) October 1st-31st 1918 Vol 37		
War Diary	L.28.b.9.9 (Sheet 36 A)	01/10/1918	01/10/1918
War Diary	Boesinghem	02/10/1918	05/10/1918
War Diary	Halloy	06/10/1918	08/10/1918
War Diary	E.22.c.29 (Sheet 57.c.N.E)	09/10/1918	10/10/1918
War Diary	L.3.b.7.2	11/10/1918	17/10/1918
War Diary	L.16.c.9.5 (Sheet 57b.NW)	18/10/1918	19/10/1918
War Diary	U.27.d.8.7 (Sheet 51.A. S.W)	20/10/1918	22/10/1918
War Diary	U.18.d.50	23/10/1918	23/10/1918
War Diary	Maison Bleue (Sheet 51A.S.E)	24/10/1918	24/10/1918
War Diary	Q.22.a.5.5	25/10/1918	26/10/1918
War Diary	Q.16.a.4.2	26/10/1918	26/10/1918
War Diary	Q.6.b.2.4	27/10/1918	27/10/1918
War Diary	Q.16.a.4.2	28/10/1918	01/11/1918
Heading	Secretary War Office (S.D.2) London		
Miscellaneous	11th Battn The Suffolk Regiment Operation Instructions Provisional		

Operation(al) Order(s)	11th Suffolks Orders No.67	02/10/1918	02/10/1918
Operation(al) Order(s)	11th Suffolks Orders No.68	05/10/1918	05/10/1918
Operation(al) Order(s)	11th Suffolks Orders No.69	08/10/1918	08/10/1918
Miscellaneous			
Operation(al) Order(s)	11th Suffolks Order No.70	17/10/1918	17/10/1918
Operation(al) Order(s)	11th Suffolks Order No.71	19/10/1918	19/10/1918
Operation(al) Order(s)	11th Suffolks Order No.72	22/10/1918	22/10/1918
Operation(al) Order(s)	11th Suffolks Order No.73	23/10/1918	23/10/1918
Operation(al) Order(s)	11th Suffolks Order No.74	25/10/1918	25/10/1918
Operation(al) Order(s)	11th Suffolks Order No.75	26/10/1918	26/10/1918
Operation(al) Order(s)	11th Suffolks Order No.77	28/10/1918	28/10/1918
Operation(al) Order(s)	11th Suffolks Order No.78	29/10/1918	29/10/1918
Operation(al) Order(s)	11th Suffolks Order No.79	30/10/1918	30/10/1918
Operation(al) Order(s)	11th Suffolks Order No.76	27/10/1918	27/10/1918
Map	Map		
Miscellaneous	Reference Sketch On Back		
Heading	War Diary 11th (S) Bn The Suffolk Regt (Camb) November 1st-30th 1918 Vol 38		
War Diary	Q.16.a.42 (Sheet 51A S.E)	01/11/1918	01/11/1918
War Diary	Somaing	01/11/1918	01/11/1918
War Diary	Avesnes-Les-Aubert	02/11/1918	07/11/1918
War Diary	Bermerain	08/11/1918	13/11/1918
War Diary	St Aubert	14/11/1918	14/11/1918
War Diary	Cambrai	15/11/1918	25/11/1918
War Diary	Heuzecourt (Lens 11)	26/11/1918	26/11/1918
War Diary	Heuzecourt	27/11/1918	30/11/1918
Operation(al) Order(s)	11th Suffolks Order No.81	01/11/1918	01/11/1918
Operation(al) Order(s)	11th Suffolks Order No.82	08/11/1918	08/11/1918
Operation(al) Order(s)	11th Suffolks Order No.83	13/11/1918	13/11/1918
Operation(al) Order(s)	11th Suffolks Order No.80	01/11/1918	01/11/1918
Miscellaneous	Special Order Of The Day By Lieut Colonel G.L.J. Tuck D.S.O. Commanding 11th Battalion The Suffolk Regt	14/11/1918	14/11/1918
Operation(al) Order(s)	11th Suffolks Order No.84	15/11/1918	15/11/1918
Operation(al) Order(s)	11th Suffolks Order No.85	22/11/1918	22/11/1918
Operation(al) Order(s)	11th Suffolks Order No.86	23/11/1918	23/11/1918
Miscellaneous	Amendment To 11th Suffolk Order No. 86	24/11/1918	24/11/1918
Miscellaneous			
Heading	War Diary 11th (S) Bn The Suffolk Regt December 1st-31st 1918 Vol 39		
War Diary	Heuzecourt	01/12/1918	06/12/1918
War Diary	Ailly-Le-Haut-Clocher (Abbeville 14)	07/12/1918	31/12/1918
Operation(al) Order(s)	11th Suffolks Order No.87	06/12/1918	06/12/1918
Heading	War Diary 11th (S) Bn The Suffolk Regt (Cambs) January 1st-31st 1919 Vol 40		
War Diary	Ailly Le Haut Clocher	01/01/1919	31/01/1919
Heading	War Diary 11th (S) Bn The Suffolk Regt (Cambs) February 1919 Vol 41		
War Diary	Ailly Le Haut Clocher	01/02/1919	11/02/1919
War Diary	Audruicq	12/02/1919	28/02/1919
Operation(al) Order(s)	11th Suffolks Order No.2	02/02/1918	02/02/1918
Heading	War Diary 11th (S) Bn The Suffolk Regt (Cambs) March 1919 Vol 42		
War Diary	Audruicq	01/03/1919	31/03/1919
Heading	War Diary April 1919 11th (S) Batt The Suffolk Regt (Cambs) Vol 43		

War Diary	Audruicq	01/04/1919	30/04/1919
Heading	War Diary May 1919 11th (S) Battn The Suffolk Regt (Cambs) Vol 44		
Miscellaneous	Memorandum	01/01/1919	01/01/1919
War Diary	Audruicq	01/05/1919	31/05/1919
Miscellaneous	O.C. 61st Divisional Units Rouen	01/07/1919	01/07/1919
Heading	War Diary June 1919 11th (S) Bn The Suffolk Regt (Cambs) Vol 45		
War Diary	Audruicq	01/06/1919	10/06/1919
War Diary	Rouen	11/06/1919	30/06/1919
Miscellaneous	Orders By Lieut Colonel G.L.J. Tuck C.M.G. D.S.O. 11th (Service) Battalion The Suffolk Regiment (Cambs)		
Heading	War Diary July 1919 11th (S) Bn The Suffolk Regt (Cambs) Vol 46		
War Diary	Rouen	01/07/1919	20/07/1919
War Diary	Duisans	21/07/1919	31/07/1919
Miscellaneous	Ceremonial Parade, Rouen, July 14th French National Fete Day	14/07/1919	14/07/1919
Miscellaneous	Orders By Major R.H. Carrette Commanding 11th (Service) Battalion The Suffolk Regiment (Cambs)	19/07/1919	19/07/1919
Miscellaneous	61st Division No.A 7615	27/07/1919	27/07/1919
Heading	War Diary August 1919 11th (S) Bn The Suffolk Regt (Cambs)		
War Diary	Arras	01/08/1919	31/08/1919
Operation(al) Order(s)	Operation Order No.1 By Lieut. Colonel C.L.J. Tuck C.M.G. D.S.O. Commanding 11th (Service) Battalion The Suffolk Regiment		
Miscellaneous	11th (Service) Battalion The Suffolk Regiment (Cambs) Table of Duties	08/08/1919	08/08/1919
Miscellaneous	Table "B" 11th (Service) Battalion The Suffolk Regiment (Cambs)		
Operation(al) Order(s)	Operation Order No.2 By Lieut. Colonel C.L.J. Tuck C.M.G. D.S.O. Commanding 11th (Service) Battalion The Suffolk Regiment		
Miscellaneous	Table "A" 11th (Service) Battalion The Suffolk Regiment (Cambs) Table Of Duties		
Heading	War Diary September 1919 11th (S) Bn The Suffolk Regt (Cambs)		
War Diary	Arras	01/09/1919	30/09/1919
Heading	War Diary 11th (S) Bn The Suffolk Regt (Cambs) October 1919		
War Diary	Arras	01/10/1919	31/10/1919
Heading	War Diary 11th (S) Bn The Suffolk Regt (Cambs) November 1919		
War Diary	Arras	01/11/1919	15/11/1919
Heading	WO95/3062-2		
Heading	61st Division 183rd Infy Bde 11th Bn Suffolk Regt Jun 1918- Nov 1919		
Miscellaneous			

WAR DIARY
or
INTELLIGENCE SUMMARY.
(Erase heading not required.)

War Diary
11th (S) Bn. The Suffolk
June 1st — 30th 1917

Place	Date	Hour	Summary of Events and Information

WAR DIARY
or
INTELLIGENCE SUMMARY.
(Erase heading not required.)

Army Form C. 2118.

Place	Date	Hour	Summary of Events and Information	Remarks and references to Appendices
LA HACQUE CAMP	1.6.18		Training in absorbing new draft. Capt C V CANNING M.C. R.S.R. over duties as Adjt vice Capt J H BRETT appointed Major.	
	2.6.18		Bn. ordered to Billets in GUARBECQUE by Hard roads. Starting point at 5.20 p.m. Arrived 7.30 p.m.	Appendix I
GUARBECQUE	3.6.18 4.6.18		Training continued.	
	5.6.18		Training continued. Platoon Exercises in Open before & offensive action. Bn. Signallers demonstration with 42nd Squadron R.A.F. with "POPHAM" Panel. Company Officers on Reconnaissance with Tanks.	
	6.6.18		Draft of 26 Officers and 70 O.R. arrived.	
	7.6.18		Training in Offensive action & Platoon Exercises. One Company in Attack & Defence Exercises in co-operation with "A" Coy. 61st M.G. Bn. Training continued. Reconnoitring parties to Front Line in ST FLORIS Sect (36A Sect 6.)	
	8.6.18		Training continued in above lines. Bn Parade for G.O.C. 183rd Inf. Bde. the G.O.C. welcomed us in new Bde & Division. Bn. Signallers demonstration with POPHAM Panel. Lt Col J H BRETT D.S.O. proceeded on command under Major J A BRETT D.S.O. Ordered to relieve 2/6 Bn R Warks Regt in left Sub Sector of ST FLORIS Sect-(Sect 36A) Starting point at 9.30 p.m. Relief completed by 1.51 a.m. System of Forward Posts with Support & Reserve Lines. 5th Division on left - Sunday L/S. CANDL.	Appendix II Appendix III
ST. FLORIS Left H.Q. (Sect 36A)	10.6.18		Quiet night. We are working hard on defences, & patrolling actively. Movement by day very restricted in this sub-section. Enemy artillery fairly active. Ours continually so.	
	11.6.18		ditto	
	12.6.18		Normal activity - always quiet, patrols active lying up in our lands. Bn Patrols locating Enemy Posts & defences.	
	13.6.18 14.6.18		ditto Normal activity. Major H P Roberts arrived & took Company Relief.	Appendix IV

Army Form C. 2118.

WAR DIARY
or
INTELLIGENCE SUMMARY.
(Erase heading not required.)

Instructions regarding War Diaries and Intelligence Summaries are contained in F. S. Regs., Part II. and the Staff Manual respectively. Title pages will be prepared in manuscript.

Place	Date	Hour	Summary of Events and Information	Remarks and references to Appendices
ST. FLORIS SECTOR (Centre)	15.6.18		Some increased artillery activity on both sides.	
	16.6.18		Normal.	
	17.6.18		Relieved by 1st Bn. E. Lancs Regt & withdrew to HAMET Billet in Bde. Reserve. Relief complete 1 a.m. All in billets 2.20 a.m.	Appendix V.
HAMET BILLET	18.6.18		Men rested and paid.	
	19.6.18		Men bathed. Two Companies on Working Party.	
	20.6.18		Two Companies on Working Party. Party of 20 officers and 190 O.R. to Bde. Reception Camp for further training. Party of 30 O.R. returned from Bde. Reception Camp.	Appendix VI.
ST. FLORIS SECTOR (Sketch 3a)	21.6.18		Relieved 9th Northumberland Fusiliers in Right Sub-section. Starting Point 10 p.m. Relief complete at 1.55 a.m. Quiet relief.	Appendix VII.
	22.6.18		This sub-section more exposed than left. No movement by day possible in forward Coys. Quiet & normal. Gas shells used by enemy during night. A day/night patrol got well forward unsuspected enemy/post.	
	23.6.18		Enemy Quiet. Our artillery active day & night. On patrols active.	
	24.6.18		Quiet. Raid operation by B Coy on right. Some retaliation on our front. Patrolling activity continued.	
	25.6.18		Gnls.- company relief. Quiet. Patrols own active by day & night.	
	26.6.18		Operation [identification] by Bn. on left (1st E.Lancs). Some retaliation on our front. Enemy artillery rather more active by day.	Appendix VIII.
	27.6.18		Enemy artillery more active on back areas - otherwise normal. Our artillery co-operating. Very little retaliation on our front. Bombing by night by R.F.A.	
	28.6.18	8 a.m.	Offensive operation by 5th Division on left - on artillery co-operating. Very little retaliation on our front. Enemy artillery more active by day & night.	
	29.6.18		Enemy quiet. Our artillery active. Enemy artillery more active by day & night.	

WAR DIARY
or
INTELLIGENCE SUMMARY.
(Erase heading not required.)

Army Form C. 2118.

Place	Date	Hour	Summary of Events and Information	Remarks and references to Appendices
ST. FLORIS SECTOR (Contd.)	30.6.18		Quiet normal. Relieved by 10th Bn E.Lancs Regt. + withdrew to MANET billet. Relief complete 1.39 a.m. "All in" MANET BILLET 2.20 a.m.	A.M.E. div IX
			Honours during month.	
			Bar to Military Cross. Major A.B. WRIGHT M.C.	
			Military Cross. Lieut. C.L. BRYANT.	
			Lieut. M.A. REED.	
			Bar to D.C.M. 14766 C.S.M. SPALDING. R.	
			D.C.M. 3/10196 C.S.M. CONNOR. C.J.	
			15/618 C.S.M. MEAD. S.W. M.M.	
			14984 Sergt. MEADOWS. F.	
			22/837 Pte MATHEWS. W.T. (now 2/Lt) M.M.	
			M.S.M. 3/10196 C.S.M. CONNOR. C.J.	
			14984 Sergt. MEADOWS. F.	
			Bar to the Military Medal. 15967 A/Cpl. SPARLE. H. M.M. Cmdg. 11th (S) Bn The Suffolk Regt.	
			Military Medal. 14877. CQMS. HYDE. F.G. 12668 Pte BUTCHER. C.	
			3/9422 Sgt. DOWE. H.	
			9717 Cpl. STADEN. S.F.	
			16988 L/Cpl DANN. P.E.	
			43483 L/Cpl GATE. T.	
			8060 Pte BUCK. W.E.	
			16447 Pte ARDHOUSE.F.	
			13012 L/Cpl CARBONNELL. F.	
			JOYCE. W.C.	
			Casualties during month.	
				Officers	O.R's
			Killed.		2
			Died of wounds.	1	1
			Wounded	2	14
			Missing	—	2
			W.Manini Major	

SECRET.   11th SUFFOLKS Operation Order   Copy No......
                No. 33.
Ref Sheet 36 A.   8.6.18.   Appendix III

1. The Battalion will relieve the 2/6th Bn Royal Warwickshire
   Regt in the left sub-sector of the ST FLORIS Sector on the night
   of 9/10th.
2. Battalion H.Qrs will be at P.5.a.3.0.
   B Company will be Right Front Coy. Coy H.Qrs at P 6 b 4 7
   D   "   "   " Left   "   "   "   " " P 6 b 4 7
   C   "   "   " Right Reserve " "   "   " P 6 a 7 4
   A   "   "   " Left   "   "   "   " " P 6 a 5 4
3. The Battn will march by platoons at 200 yards distance along
   GUARBECQUE-ST VENANT Road to Road junction P.9.b.8.9. where
   guides will be met.
   Order of march. :   A,C,D,B Coys and Bn.H.Qrs.
   Starting point. Drawbridge by A Coy.
   Time.   9.30 p.m.
   Dress : Fighting Order,S.B.Respirators at the ALERT position.
4. Advance parties of Intelligence Officer,Sniping Corpl,
   2 H.Qrs Signallers ,1 Officer per Coy,1 N.C.O. per platoon,
   No.1 of L.G.teams,1 Signaller and 1 runner per Coy. will
   parade at 8 p.m. tonight in Fighting Kit with rations for
   tomorrow and proceed as already detailed.
5. B Coy will arrange to relieve the guard at No.6.Bridge
   at P.4.b.1.1. by 6 p.m.tomorrow.
6. All Liason duties at present found by 2/6th Warwicks
   will be carefully taken over.
7. All aeroplane photos,paper maps,Gas and trench stores,
   and S.O.S.Grenades will be taken over and receipts given.
   Lists of articles so taken over to be forwarded to Bn.H.Qrs
   within 12 hours of relief. Receipts will be signed by both
   parties.
8. The T.O. will arrange to collect Lewis Guns,Packs and
   baggage etc from Coy H.Qrs ,Orderly Room and Mess as already
   detailed.
   Baggage for Q.M.Stores to be ready by 8.30 p.m.
      "   "   the Line.   "   "   " 9 p.m.
9. Rations for B and D Coys will be brought up cooked ,for
   Bn.H.Qrs ,A and C Coys uncooked. Water will be brought up
   in petrol tins which on no account will be punctured or
   burnt.
10. Completion of relief will be reported by the code word
    "CANAL".
11. ACKNOWLEDGE.

                                        Captain & A/Adjutant.
                                        11th SUFFOLKS.

       Copies No.s.1 and 2.   Retained.
              3 - 6   Coy.
                7.   T.O.
                8.   Q.M.
                9.   Sig Off.
               10.   R.S.M.
               11   2/6th Warwicks.

SECRET Copy No. 1

11th SUFFOLKS OPERATION ORDER
No. 35.
12.6.18.

Appendix IV

Reference 36.A.
36.A.S.E.

1. The following inter-company reliefs will take place on the night 13/14th June 1918.-
    A.Coy. will relieve D.Coy. and become Left Front Company
    C. "   ..   .. B. "   ..   .. Right "   "
    D. "   will be Left Support Company
    B. "   .. .. Right ..   "

2. 1 N.C.O. per Platoon will be sent to their respective new Areas on the night 12/13th June.

3. All Trench Stores, etc. will be handed over.
   Work in hand will be carefully explained.

4. Completion of relief will be notified to Battn.H.Q. by Code phrase "No more spirit wanted".

5. ACKNOWLEDGE.

Copies No.1 & 2 Retained.
   "   3 - 6 Coys.   Captain and Adjutant,
   "   7. Q.M.& T.O.   11th Bn.THE SUFFOLK REGT.
   "   8. S.O.& R.S.M.
   "   9. O.C.Right Bn.
   "   10. " 478 Coy.R.E.
   "   11. " Left Group R.F.A.
   "   12. " M.G.Bn.

Issued at 10 p.m.

SECRET.
Appendix V
Copy No. 1

11th SUFFOLKS OPERATION ORDER
No. 38.   16.6.18.

Reference Sheet 36.A.

1. The 1st E.Lancs.Regt. will relieve the Battalion in the left Section ST FLORIS SECTOR, on the night of the 17/18th inst.
   A.Coy. will be relieved by B.Coy. of the E.Lancs.
   B.   "   "   "   "   " C. "   "   "   "
   C.   "   "   "   "   " D. "   "   "   "
   D.   "   "   "   "   " A. "   "   "   "

2. Order of Relief. – A., C., D., & B.Coys. and Battn.H.Qs.
   On relief the Battalion will withdraw to HAMET BILLET and be in Brigade Reserve.

3. 1 Officer per Coy., 1 N.C.O. per Platoon, No. 1's of Lewis Gun teams and a proportion of Signallers and Runners of the 1st E.Lancs. Regt. will come into the line on the night of the 16/17th inst., and take over all Stores etc.

4. All Aeroplane Photographs, Paper Maps etc. will be handed over. Lists of Trench Stores handed over will be sent to the Orderly Room by 9 a.m. the 17th inst.

5. GUIDES. 1 Guide per Platoon and Coy.H.Qs., and 1 Guide for Battn. H.Q. will report to 2/Lieut. F.E.Catchpole at Road Junction, P.v.b.9.5 at 10.30 p.m. on the 17th inst.
   1 Guide per Post for the Front Coys. will meet incoming Platoons at their respective Coy. H.Qs.

6. Completion of relief will be notified to Battn. H.Qs. by the Code Word "HAPPY".
   Arrival in HAMET BILLET will be notified to Battn. H.Qs. by the Code Word "HEAVEN".

7. One N.C.O. per Coy. and Battn. H.Qs. will proceed to HAMET BILLET and report to Capt. & Q.M. C.McD.Lindsey at the Battn.H.Qs. of the 1st E.Lancs. at 6 p.m. on the 17th inst.
   Coys. will take over the Billets of the relieving Coys.

8. ACKNOWLEDGE.

Issued at 5.30 p.m.

Captain and Adjutant,
11th Battn. THE SUFFOLK REGT.

Copy No.1 & 2 Retained.
   3 – 6 Companies.
   7. Sig. Officer.
   8. Intelligence Officer.
   9. Quartermaster.
   10. Transport Officer.
   11. R.S.M.
   12. 1st E.Lancs.

Appendix VII

Copy No. 1

SECRET.

11th SUFFOLKS OPERATION ORDER
No. 38.

20.6.18.

Ref. Sheet 36.A.
36.A. N.E.
36.A. S.E.

1. The Battalion will relieve the 9th Northumberland Fusiliers in the Right Subsection of the ST FLORIS Section on the night of the 21/22nd inst.
2. B.Coy. will be Right Front Company.
   D. " " " Left " "
   A. " " " in Support.
   C. " " " Reserve.
3. Order of March - D, B, A, C and Battn. H.Qs.
4. 1 Officer, 1 runner and 1 Signaller per Company, 1 N.C.O. per Platoon, No. 1's of Lewis Gun Teams, 2 Runners, 2 Signallers and Intelligence Officer from Battn. H.Qs. will go into the line on the night of 20/21st inst. This party will parade at O.R. at 9.30 p.m. ready to proceed to the trenches.
5. All Aeroplane Photos, paper maps etc will be taken over. Lists of Trench Stores taken over will be forwarded to O.R. by 3.30 a.m. 22nd inst.
6. No movement in connection with the relief will take place before 10 p.m. and all movement by Platoons at 300 yards interval.
7. GUIDES. 1 Guide per Coy. will report to Battn. Orderly Room HAMET BILLET on night 20/21st for Advance Party.
   1 Guide per Platoon and Coy. H.Qs. and one per Battn.H.Qs. will report to O.R. HAMET BILLET on night of 21/22nd.
8. Relief complete will be notified to Battn. H.Qs. by the code words "NO SHOVELS REQUIRED".
9. Transport Officer will arrange for Lewis Gun Limbers and Limbers for Officers Trench Kit and Mess Kit to be at respective Coy. H.Qs. by 9 p.m.
10. ACKNOWLEDGE.

Captain and Adjutant,
11th Battalion THE SUFFOLK REGIMENT.

Copy No. 1 & 2 Retained.
3 - 6 Coys.
7. Transport Officer.
8. Quartermaster.
9. Headquarters
10. R.S.M.
11. 9th N.F.

Appendix VIII

S.E.T. Copy No......

11th Bn.THE SUFFOLK REGIMENT ORDER No.30.

24-6-16.

Reference Sheet 36.A.

1. The following inter-company reliefs will take place on the night 25/26th June 1916 :-
   C.Coy. will relieve B.Coy. and become Right Front Company.
   A. "   "   "   D. "   "   "   Left   "   "
   D. "   "   be Support Company.
   B. "   "   " Reserve   "

2. All details of relief and necessary reconnaissance will be made direct by Company Commanders concerned.

3. One N.C.O. per Platoon will be sent to their respective new areas on the night 24/25th June.

4. All Trench Stores etc., and Work in hand will be carefully handed over.

5. Completion of relief and arrival in new areas will be notified to Battn.H.Qs. by the following code :-
   A.Company. "ACCOUNT SETTLED."
   B.   "   "REVETTING FINISHED."
   C.   "   "ALL PARTICULARS TAKEN."
   D.   "   "WORK IN HAND."

6. No movement in connection with relief before 10 p.m.

7. Acknowledge.

Issued at 10 a.m.

Copy No.1. War Diary.
        2. File.
        3 - 6 Companies.
        7. Q.M.
        8. M.O.
        9. Off.i/c Bn.H.Qs.
        10. A/R.S.M.
        11.   " Right.Bn.
        12.   " Left.Bn.
        13. Right Group R.F.A.

Capt. Canning

Capt.in and Adjutant,
11th Bn.THE SUFFOLK REGIMENT.

Army Form C. 2118.

WAR DIARY
or
INTELLIGENCE SUMMARY.

(Erase heading not required.)

War Diary
11th (S.) Bn. The Suffolk Regt. (Cambs)
July 1st — 31st 1918.

WAR DIARY
or
INTELLIGENCE SUMMARY.
(Erase heading not required.)

Army Form C. 2118.

Place	Date	Hour	Summary of Events and Information	Remarks and references to Appendices
MMET BILLET.	1.7.18		Men rested – cleaning up after form in line.	
	2.7.18		Bn. ordered to reorganise under G.H.Q. letter O.B/1919 of 14 June 1918.	
	3.7.18		Re-organising. 2 Coys. on working Party.	
	4.7.18		Interchange of men & training at Bn. Reception Camp. 2 Coys. on working Party.	
ST FLORIS SECTOR Left Sub-Section	5.7.18		Relieve 9th Bn Northumberland Fusiliers in left sub-sector of ST FLORIS SECTOR. Starting Point 8.10 p.m. Relief complete 1.15 a.m. On our Coy Sub. artillery active by night. Enemy using a large number of parachute lights.	Appendix I
	6.7.18		Quiet relief. All set to be concentrated on supporting trials & continuous throughout Bde. front. Enemy artillery more active at night harassing fire during last hour.	
	7.7.18		Offensive operation. Recover identification on our front by 9th Northumberland Fusiliers. Zero hour 10 a.m. No prisoners. Enemy retaliation almost nil. Inter- Coy. relief. complete by 2 a.m. Enemy night harassing fire active. Offensive operation to obtain identification by Bn. on left. Zero 11 p.m. No prisoners.	Appendix II
	8.7.18		5 officers & 100 O.R. from detail at Bn. Reception Camp. to take part Offensive operation. Recover identification by Bde. on night. On artillery co-operating. No prisoners. Advance parties of 7th Division reconnoitring line.	Appendix III
	9.7.18		Normal. Our patrols active and prowling.	

Army Form C. 2118.

WAR DIARY
or
INTELLIGENCE SUMMARY.
(Erase heading not required.)

Instructions regarding War Diaries and Intelligence Summaries are contained in F.S. Regs., Part II. and the Staff Manual respectively. Title pages will be prepared in manuscript.

Place	Date	Hour	Summary of Events and Information	Remarks and references to Appendices
ST-FLORIS SECTOR	10.7.18		Quiet. Some harassing fire by enemy artillery 10 – 12 MN.	
ST.HILAIRE	11.7.18		Relieved by 10th Bn. K.S.L.I. (23rd Inf.Bde. 7th Div.) Relief complete 2.15 a.m. On relief Division in G.H.Q. Reserve, and march to billets in ST.HILAIRE. Arrived in billets at 7.50 a.m.	Appendix IV.
	12.7.18		Rest, Inspections, etc.	
	13.7.18		Training started. Six new Officers joined.	
	14.7.18		Bds. Church Parade, attended by Army Commander. 2 hour officers parade. Inspection of billets.	
	15.7.18		Men bathed. Training programme attacked for first week.	Appendix V.
	16.7.18		Training continued.	
LINGHEM	17.7.18		Ordered to LINGHEM area, by March Route. Starting point 9.30 a.m. arrived 10.45 a.m.	Appendix VI
	18.7.18		Training continued. Night operations – "marching to an assembly position."	
	19.7.18		Training continued. Preliminary Defence orders issued.	Appendix VII
	20.7.18		Training continued.	
	21.7.18		Training continued.	
	22.7.18		Church Parade Memorial Service. Programme of Sports for week attached.	Appendix VIII
CAMPAGNE (Sect 2?)	23.7.18		Ordered to HERINGHEM – CAMPAGNE Area A to join XV Corps, by March Route. Starting point 11 a.m. Arrived in billets at 7.30 p.m. at CAMPAGNE.	Appendix IX
	24.7.18		Reconnaissance of line by C.O. + Coy. Cmdrs. Inspection of billets.	Appendix X
	25.7.18		Training continued. Preliminary defence orders issued.	
	26.7.18		Training continued.	
	27.7.18			

WAR DIARY
or
INTELLIGENCE SUMMARY.
(Erase heading not required.)

Army Form C. 2118.

Place	Date	Hour	Summary of Events and Information	Remarks and references to Appendices
CAMPAGNE	28.7.18		Programme of training week attacked.	Appendix XV / Appendix XVI
	29.7.18		Bn in Reserve. Defence Inhabitants "A" viewed.	
	30.7.18		Bn Scheme.	
	31.7.18		Ordered to LINGHEM area to South March. Starting Point 9×8 pm.	Appendix XVII
		3.15 am.	Arrived 1st Aug.	
			Casualties during month.	
			Killed. Wounded.	
			Officers. — 1	
			O.R's. 2 3.	

E.L. Tuck. Lieut Col.
Cmdg. 11th Bn Suffolk Regt.
1.8.18.

Appendix I

SECRET.   11th SUFFOLKS ORDER No. 42.   Copy No. 7

Ref Sheet 36A.   3.7.17.

1. The Battalion will relieve the 9th (N.H) Bn Northumberland Fusiliers in the left sub-section of the ST FLORIS SECTOR on the night of 4/5th July.
   B Company will be Right front Company.
   D   "   "   " Left   "
   C   "   "   " in Support.
   A   "   "   " in Reserve.

2. No movement in connection with relief will take place before 10 p.m. and all movement will be by platoons at 200 yds distance. Order of March.   D,B,C,A and H.Qrs.

3. 1 Officer per Company will go into the line on the night of 3/4th inst.

4. GUIDES will be met as follows :-
   1 per Post for D Company at road junction P.5.e.5.2. and proceed by Canal Bank.
   1 Per Post for B Company at Road Junction P.5.e.5.2. and proceed by ST FLORIS Road.
   1 Per Platoon for C Company at road junction P.5.e.5.2. and proceed by Canal Bank.
   1 Per Platoon for A Company at road Junction P.5.e.5.2. and proceed by ST FLORIS ROAD.

5. All aeroplane photos, maps, Hot food containers, etc will be taken over. Lists of Trench Stores taken over will be forwarded to O.R. by 8 a.m. 5th inst.

6. Relief complete will be notified to Bn H.Qrs by the following code words :-
   A Company.   ACKNOWLEDGED.
   B   "   BATMAN WANTED.
   C   "   CHAMPION SGT.
   D   "   DOG REQUIRED.

7. Transport Officer will arrange for limber for Lewis Guns and limber for Officers trench kits, Mess Kit, O.R.Boxes etc to be at respective Coy H.Q. at 9 p.m.
   All stores returning to transport and Q.M.Stores will be stacked by Orderly Room ready for loading at 9 p.m.
   Sgt Fitzgerald and 2 men will remain with these stores until collected.

8. ACKNOWLEDGE.

                                    C Manning
                                    Captain & Adjutant.
                                    11th Bn The SUFFOLK Regt.

Copies Nos. 1 and 2   Retained.
       3 " 6   Coys.
         7   T.O.
         8   Q.M.
         9   H.Qrs and R.S.M.
        10   9th N.F.

X 1 per Bn Snipers & Observers at Road junc. P.5.e.5.2 & proceed by ST FLORIS ROAD.

PROGRAMME OF WORK.

Appendix I

SUNDAY   Church Parade.
                                    Ceremonial.
                                    Inspection of Billets.

MONDAY.   8 - 8.30 a.m.   Inspections.
           8.30 - 9.30 a.m.   Section and Platoon Drill.
           9.30 - 10.30 a.m.   4 half Coys. B.T.& P.T.) followed
                                    4 half Coys. Musketry.) by games.
           10.30 - 10.45 a.m.   Talk.
           10.45 - 11 a.m.   Break.
           11 - 12 noon.   4 half Coys. B.F.& P.T.
                                    4 half Coys. Musketry.
           12 - 12.15 p.m.   March to Bn. Parade Ground.
           12.15 - 12.45 p.m.   Battalion Drill.
           12.45 - 1 p.m.   March Discipline on way to Billets.
           2 - 3 p.m.   Officers and Sergts.
                                    Lewis Gun Instruction.
           3 - 5 p.m.   Recreational Training.
           5.30 p.m.   Lecture to Officers and Sergts.

TUESDAY.   8 - 8.30 a.m.   Inspections.
           8.30 - 9.30 a.m.   Section and Platoon Drill.
           9.30 - 10.30 a.m.   4 half B.F.& P.T.   ) followed
                                    4 half Coys. Musketry   ) by games.
           10.30 - 10.45 a.m.   Talks.
           10.45 - 11 a.m.   Break.
           11 - 12 noon   4 half Coys. B.F.& P.T.
                                    4 half Coys. Musketry.
           12 - 12.15 p.m.   March to Battn. Parade Ground.
           12.15 - 12.45 p.m.   Battalion Drill.
           12.45 - 1 p.m.   March Discipline on the way to Billets.
           2 - 3 p.m.   Officers and Sergts.
                                    Lewis Gun Instruction.
           3 - 5 p.m.   Recreational Training.
           10 - 11 p.m.   Forming up by night.

WEDNESDAY. 8 - 8.30 a.m.   Inspections.
           8.30 - 9.30 a.m.   Section and Platoon Drill.
9-30 - 10-30   4 half Coys. B.F.& P.T.) followed
                                    4 half Coys. Musketry   ) Musketry.
           10.30 - 10.45 a.m.   Talk.
           10.45 - 11 a.m.   Break.
           11 - 12 noon.   4 half Coys. B.F.& P.T.
                                    4 half Coys. Musketry.
           12 - 12.15 p.m.   March to Battn. Parade Ground.
           12.15 - 12.45 p.m.   Battalion Drill.
           12.45 - 1 p.m.   March Discipline on way to Billets.
           2 - 3 p.m.   Officers and Sergts.
                                    Lewis Gun Instruction.
           3 - 5 p.m.   Recreational Training.
           5.30 p.m.   Lecture on "Espirit de Corps" by
                                    Captain R.Le Fanu, Bde Major, 183 Bde.

THURSDAY. 8 - 8.30 a.m.   Inspections.
           8.30 - 9.30 a.m.   Section and Platoon Drill.
           9.30 - 10.30 a.m.   4 half Coys. B.F.& P.T.) followed
                                    4 half Coys. Musketry.) by games.
           10.30 - 10.45 a.m.   Talk.
           10.45 - 11 a.m.   Break.
           11 - 12 noon.   4 half Coys. B.F.& P.T.
                                    4 half Coys. Musketry.
           12 - 12.15 p.m.   March to Battn. Parade Ground.
           12.15 - 12.45 p.m.   Battalion Drill.
           12.45 - 1 p.m.   March Discipline on way to Billets.
           2 - 3 p.m.   Officers and Sergts.
                                    Lewis Gun Instruction.
           3 - 5 p.m.   Recreational Training.
           5.30 p.m.   Lecture.

xxxxxxx

---2---

FRIDAY.	8 - 8.30 a.m.	Inspections.
	8.30 - 9.15 a.m.	Platoon and Coy. Drill.
	9.15 - 10 a.m.	1 Coy. Extended Order Drill.
		1 Coy. Patrolling.
		2 Half Coys. B.F.& P.T.
		2 Half Coys. Musketry.
	10 - 10.15 a.m.	Talk.
	10.15 - 10.30 a.m.	Break.
	10.30 - 11.15 a.m.	1 Coy. Extended Order Drill.
		1 Coy. Patrolling.
		2 Half Coys. B.F.& P.T.
		2 Half Coys. Musketry.
	11.15 - 12 noon.	4 Half Coys. B.F.& P.T.
		4 Half Coys. Musketry.
	12 - 12.15 p.m.	March to Battn. Parade Ground.
	12.15 - 12.45 p.m.	Battalion Drill.
	12.45 - 1 p.m.	March discipline on way to Billets.
	2 - 3 p.m.	Officers and Sergts.
		Lewis Gun Instruction.
	3 - 5 p.m.	Recreational Training.
	10 - 11 p.m.	Advancing by night.
SATURDAY.	8 - 8.30 a.m.	Inspections.
	8.30 - 9.15 a.m.	Platoon and Coy. Drill.
	9.15 - 10 a.m.	1 Coy. Extended Order Drill
		1 Coy. Patrolling.
		2 half Coys. B.F.& P.T.
		2 half Coys. Musketry.
	10 - 10.15 a.m.	Talk.
	10.15 - 10.30 a.m.	Break.
	10.30 - 11.15 a.m.	1 Coy. Extended Order Drill
		1 Coy. Patrolling.
		2 half B.F.& P.T.
		2 half Coys. Musketry.
	11.15 - 12 noon.	4 half Coys. B.F.& P.T.
		4 half Coys. Musketry.
	12 - 12.15 p.m.	March to Battn. Parade Ground.
	12.15 - 12.45 p.m.	Battalion Drill.
	12.45 - 1 p.m.	March Discipline on way to Billets.
	2 - 3 p.m.	Officers and Sergts.
		Lewis Gun Instruction.
	3 - 5 p.m.	Recreational Training.

A proportion of all Drill, Musketry and Marching will be done in Gas Masks.

12:7:18.

Lieut.Colonel,
Comdg. 11th Battalion THE SUFFOLK REGT.

Appendix II

SECRET.

11th SUFFOLKS ORDER No. 64.   Copy No......
In conjunction with 101 Bde Order No.58.

6.7.16.

1. Tonight 6/7th July, Fighting Patrols of 9th Bn The Northumberland Fusiliers, will raid the enemy trenches South of OVILLERS between the ST ELOI - OVILLERS Road and the Railway and secure identification.
   The objective and limit of advance will be the actual line U.S.d.25.30. - U.S.a.15.30.

2. The Raid will be supported by Artillery - Trench Mortar and Machine Gun Fire.
   All fire will cease at Zero plus 30 minutes.

3. Raiding patrols will be formed up ready outside our wire at Zero minus 5 minutes. At Zero they will advance on the objective.

4. Zero hour will be 1 a.m.

5. The Signal for withdrawal will be Red Very Lights.

6. A Forward Aid Post will be established at the Right Front Coy H.Qrs, which must be cleared of all unnecessary personnel.

7. O.C."D" Coy will detail 2 S.B.'s with 1 Stretcher to report to O.C.B Coy at 11.30 p.m. These with the 4 S.B.'s of B Coy (with 2 stretchers) will be in front line by 20 mns, and will carry any Raid casualties to Forward Aid Post (at Front Coy H.Q.)

8. O.C.C Coy and O.C.A Coy will each detail 2 bearers (with 1 Stretcher) to report to Forward Aid Post (Right Front Coy H.Q.) by 11.30 p.m. These bearers will carry any raid casualties from Forward Aid Post to R.A.P.

9. A limber with two bridges will report to O.C.B Coy at 10.30 p.m. He will see these handed over to Raiding Party.

10. Rendezvous for raiding party will be the WHITE HOUSE.
    O.C. A Coy will supply raiding party with 12 Boxes Grenades (Mills No.5.) by 10.30 p.m.
    O.C. A Coy will also arrange for cooks of 9th N.F. to prepare tea in the WHITE HOUSE for the return of the raiders.

11. ACKNOWLEDGE.

C Fanning
Captain & Adjutant.
11th SUFFOLKS.

Copy No.1 and 2   Retained.
     3 - 6   Coys.

SECRET.   Appendix IV
                                            Copy No. ....

            11th SUFFOLKS ORDER No. 46.
            ----------oOo----------   10:7:18.

Reference Sheet 28.A.

1.   The 10th Battalion K.S.L.I.(61st.Bde.) will relieve the Battalion in
the Left Sub-section ST FLORIS SECTOR, on the night 10/11th inst.
     On completion of relief the Battalion will withdraw to the ST HILAIRE
- BOURECQ Area, and be in G.H.Q. Reserve.

2.   On relief the Battalion will march to GUARBECQUE by Platoons at 100
yards interval, and rendezvous at P.11.d.90.40 where breakfast will be
served.

3.   The Bridge Guard at P.4.b.10.10 found by B.Coy. will be relieved by
6 p.m. 10th inst. On relief this guard will report to Battalion H.Q.

4.   All Documents, Paper Trench Maps,(including Secret Maps issued by the
Division), Aeroplane Photos, and all other Trench Stores will be handed
over on relief. Coys. will forward to Battalion H.Qrs. by 6 p.m.,10th inst
list of Stores they are handing over.
     C.Coy. will hand over Stores on Forward R.E.Material Dump.
     B. "   "   "   "   "   in Battn.Cookhouses, & at Coy. H.Qrs.
     A/R.S.M. "   "   "   "   on Battn.Dump and on Left, Left Centre
                                  and White Hou se Dumps.
Any broken Tools must be handed over and shown as such. Each Coy. will
hand over 12 Petrol Tins, Bn.H.Qs. 6 and Transport Officer 24. Remainder
of Mobile Reserve will be carried out.
     Printed Maps, scales 1/20,000, 1/40,000 and 1/80,000 will not be
handed over.

5.   Guides at the rate of 1 per Coy. H.Qs., 1 per Platoon and one per Bn.
H.Qs. will report to Lieut.C.J.Mason at Cross Roads P.7.b.90.90 at 10.30
p.m. on 10th inst.
     C. and D.Coy. guides will lead in relieving troops by the ST FLORIS
Road. A. and B.Coy. guides will lead in relieving troops by CANAL BANK.
     Guides at the rate of 1 per Post for front Coys. will meet incoming
Platoons as under :-
          C.Coy. 2 guides at Coy. H.Qs.
          A. "   "   "   on CANAL BANK at P.8.b.70.80.

6.   Completion of relief will be signed to Battn.H.Q. by the following
code words :-   A.Coy.   "ESTABLISHMENT ADEQUATE."
                B. "   "ESTABLISHMENT RAW."
                C. "   "ESTABLISHMENT CORRECT."
                D. "   "ESTABLISHMENT DEFICIENT."

7.   Transport Officer will arrange for 1 limber to be at Aid Post for
Coy.Mess Kit, Cooks Kit, Officers Trench Kit, Aid Post and Orderly Room
Boxes at 11 p.m., and 3 limbers for bombs etc. by Cross Roads P.7.b.97.90
at 12 midnight.
     Transport Officer will detail Cookers, Lewis Gun limbers, Pack Ani-
mals, and Officers Chargers to be at Battn. Headquarts at P.d. 1131 inst

- 2 -

Remainder of Transport will march under Transport Officer to new area under orders to be issued by the B.T.O. Transport will move complete with ammunition and tools, and a certificate rendered to Staff Captain, repeated to Battn.H.Qs., that this has been done.

Baggage Wagons will join Transport under orders issued by O.C.Trains

8. The following Officers and N.C.Os. will remain in the line with 10th Bn.K.S.L.I. until such time as their services are no longer required :-
   Lieut. S.J. Mason)
   2/Lieut. D. Ros.) with Battalion H.Qs.
   Corpl. W. Ross, DCM, MM)
   L/Corpl. H. Greenwood.)
   2 N.C.Os. per Company.

9. 2/Lieut.P.H.Mothersole, MM, with Billeting Party will report to Rear Bde. H.Qs., HERRINTHE at 9.30 a.m. 10th inst. where lorry will convey them to new area. On arrival he will meet Billet Warden at Y.M.C.A. Hut ST HILAIRE at 11 a.m.

10. Medical Officer will notify A.D.M.S., reporting to Battn.H.Qs., any cases of P.U.Os. unable to move with Battalion, for transfer to Detention Camp at TINCHEBRAI.

11. One lorry which may do two journeys will report to Rear Bde. H.Qs. at 1.30 p.m. on 10th inst. to assist in move. Quartermasters will arrange for a guide to be at above H.Qs. by 1.30 p.m. to guide lorry to Q.M.Stores

12. Quartermaster will arrange for breakfast to be served on arrival of Battalion at rendezvous, and for details to rejoin Coys. at same time and place. He will report personally to Commanding Officer at rendezvous

13. Acknowledge.

Issued at 3 a.m.
Captain and Adjutant,
11th Bn. THE SUFFOLK REGIMENT. (CAMBS).

Copy No. 1 & 2 Retained.
 3 - 6 Companies.
 7. H.Q.
 8. Q.M.
 9. T.O.
 10. I.O.
 11. A/R.S.M.
 12. 10th Bn.K.S.L.I.
 13. 103rd Bde. H.Qn.

SECRET.

Appendix VI
Copy No........

11th SUFFOLKS ORDER No. 47.

15.7.18.

Reference Sheet 36.A.

1. The Battalion will move to LINGHEM tomorrow and take over Billets from 2/4th Royal Berkshire Regt.

2. Battalion Parade on Football Ground, T.5.d.3.3 at 6.40 a.m. Transport on the Main Road in T.5.c. facing N.E. with head at Football Ground.
Dress - Full Marching Order. Steel Helmets will be worn.

3. The Battalion will move with a distance of 100 yards between Coys and between the rear Coy. and Transport.
The Transport will march with 25 yards distance between each six vehicles.
The two L.Gun Limbers of each Coy. will march with their Coys.

4. Route - Fork Roads T.5.d.4.9 - NORRENT FONTES - Fork Roads N.29.c.8.1 - ROMBLY.

5. Breakfast - 7.15 a.m.
Sick Parade - 8 a.m. (Sick will bring full marching order.)

6. All baggage, Officers Valises, etc. to be ready outside Coy. and Battn. H.Qs. for collection by the Transport at 8.15 a.m.

7. Billets to be ready for inspection by 8.30 a.m.

8. ACKNOWLEDGE.

CAPTAIN AND ADJUTANT,
11TH BATTALION THE SUFFOLK REGIMENT.

Copy No.1 & 2 Retained.
3 - 6 Companies.
7. Battn. H.Qs.
8. Quartermaster.
9. Transport Officer.
10. R.S.M.
11. 183rd Brigade H.Qs.

Issued at 7 p.m.

S E C R E T.

11th Battalion THE SUFFOLK REGT.   Appendix VI

DEFENCE INSTRUCTIONS No.1.

Reference Sheet 36.A.

1. The Battalion is in G.H.Q. Reserve and as such may be called upon :
   (a) To move from the XI Corps Area.
   (b) To act as XI Corps Reserve in the event of an attack.
2. In accordance with above the formation of Brigade Groups may be necessary, and will take place on receipt of the order "FORM BRIGADE GROUP".
3. In the event of the order Form Brigade Group being issued, the undermentioned will form the 183rd Infantry Brigade (LINGHAM BRIGADE) Group :

   183rd Infantry Brigade.
   No.3 Sec.61 Div.Sig.Coy.
   "B" Coy. 61st Bn.M.G.C.
   478 Field Coy. R.E.
   2/1st Field Ambulance.
   No.3 Coy.61 Div.Train.

4. Major A.B.Wright, M.C. will proceed to and report at Bde. H.Qs. FONTES for instructions.
5. The Battalion will be ready to move at short notice in Fighting Order.
6. Acknowledge.

                                          Captain and Adjutant,
                                    11th Battalion THE SUFFOLK REGIMENT.

19:7:18.

        Copy No.1   C.O.
             2   2nd in Command.
             3 - 4 File.
             5 - 8 Companies.
             9   Battn. H.Qs.
            10   Q.M.
            11   T.O.
            12   R.S.M.
            13.   183rd Brigade.

Appendix VII

SECRET.   11th Battalion The SUFFOLK REGIMENT.

DEFENCE INSTRUCTIONS No.2.

Sheet 36.A.

1. In the event of the Battalion having to move from XI Corps Area the move will take place either :-
   (a) by March Route.
   (b) by Train.
   (c) by Bus.
   (d) by a combination of a, b, and c.
   In all cases the move will be by Bde Group.

2. (a) In case of 1 (a) Route will be detailed when destination is known.
   (b) In case of 1 (b) if move takes place by strategical trains, the whole of the Bde Group will move by rail.
   Probable entraining stations are AIRE or WIZERNES (3½ miles S. by W. of ST OMER.
   (c) In case of 1 (c) probable embussing places are N.29.c.7.0. - N.23.a.3.9. on the ST HILAIRE-AVCHY AU-BOIS ROAD.

3. ACKNOWLEDGE.

19.7.18.   Capt and Adjutant.
                                        11th SUFFOLK Regt.

Copy No.1.   C.O.
     2.   2nd in Command.
     3 - 4   File.
     5 - 8   Coys.
     9.   Bn H.Qrs.
     10.   Q M.
     11.   T.O.
     12.   R.S.M.
     13.   183rd Brigade.

SECRET.   11th (S) Bn The SUFFOLK REGIMENT.   Appendix VII
           DEFENCE INSTRUCTIONS No.3.

Ref. Sheet 36 A. (The Div. acting as XI Corps Reserve in case
                                              of attack.)

1. On the order "EMBUS LEFT" the Bde plus B Coy 61st Bn M.G.C
   will be prepared to carry out :
       (1) To extend the Left flank of XI Corps from ESB GD DAM
       (K.9.a.4.0.) along the BOURRE RIVER and the BRAS DE LA BOURRE
       (K.9.a.-E.25.d.-D.14.)
       (2) To extend the Left flank of XI Corps from LA MOTTE-AU
       -BOIS along the canal running through D.12 and D.11.
       (3) To counter attack N.E. to drive the enemy back across
       the canal in D.12. and D.11.
2. The Bde concentration area will be Area "L" STEENBECQUE-
   BOISEGHEM-THIENNES.
3. The move to this area will be by lorry in accordance
   with attached table. Coys marching independently to
   starting point N.21.a.8.7. Debussing point, head of column
   I.7.d.6.4. Major.J.H.Brett will superintend embussing of
   the Battalion and will ensure that convoy is properly
   parked each evening. The Battalion will embus and move
   off at one hours notice.
4. Lewis and Vickers Guns will be taken in the lorries.
5. On arrival at STEENBECQUE A and B Coys will proceed as an
   advanced guard to undermentioned important tactical localities
   and relieve the nucleus garrisons of Cyclists and Corps
   Cavalry (K.E.H.)   A Coy to DENISE FARM locality J.2.c.
                       B Coy to DELEGATE FARM locality J.1.b.
   ½ Section of 61st Divl M.G.C. will proceed with both A and B
   Coys and be under their Command.
B. A Coy will on arrival, establish touch with nucleus garrisons
   of troops of XV Corps about the level crossing in D.25.
A. B Coy will gain touch with a platoon of XI Corps Cyclists
   at point where light railway passes through BUSNES-STEENBECQUE
   line in J.14.c.
   The tasks of the above garrisons are :-
       (1) To collect and reform any troops falling back on their
   localities.
       (2) To act as guides to reinforcing troops.
       (3) In event of a rapid enemy advance to create a block
   until such time as reinforced.
   They will be available to move forward with the Bn for
   offensive or other operations forward. The Bn less A and B
   Coys will bivouac in fields along road running between
   I.5.d.70.65 and I.12.a.30.70.
6. Capt.C.V.Canning.M.C. will report to Bde Report Centre
   I.8.b.6.1. as soon as Bn arrives in concentration area.
7. Surplus personnel will remain at LINGHEM. Coys and H.Qrs
   will at once prepare a detail of Fighting and Surplus personnel
   and forward his rolls to the Orderly Room.
8. (a) Transport will proceed independently and assemble
   in fields at H.29.d. and H.28.b. The T.O. will detail
   guide to report to the Staff Capt at the Cross Roads H.28.b.5.7

   (b) Baggage wagons will report to Units. As soon as
   loaded 1 per Bn will return to its train Coy.
   The second wagon will be returned to Train Coy loaded as
   soon as Bn is in a position to do so.
   All surplus Kit will be sent to Adjutant of the Reception
   Camp for storage. B Coy will detail an elderly man to
   remain as guard of this dump. He will be supplied with 3
   days rations.
   (c) All moves of Transport and Q.M.Stores will at once
   be reported to Staff Captain.
   Q.M. will arrange for 4 Orderlies (cyclists or mounted)
   to remain with Q.M.Stores and transport whose duty will be
   to keep touch and notify any change of location. He will

PROGRAMME OF WORK.   Appendix VIII.

SUNDAY. 21st		Church Parade. Ceremonial. Inspection of billets.	
MONDAY. 22nd	8 - 8.30 a.m.	Inspections.	
	8.30 - 11.30 a.m.	Route March. Lesson in use of ground during interval.	
	2 - 3 p.m.	L.G.Instruction for Offs and Sergts.	
	3 - 5 p.m.	Recreational Training.	
	5.30 p.m.	Lecture.	
	10 - 11.30 p.m.	Night Advance and attack.	A.
TUESDAY. 23rd	8 - 8.30 a.m.	Inspections.	
	8.30 - 8.45 a.m.	March to Ranges.	
	8.45 - 9.45 a.m.	2 Coys Musketry including range work.	E
		2 Coys P.T., work in Small Box Respirators and talk	F K
	9.45 - 10.45 a.m.	2 Coys Musketry including Range work.	E
		2 Coys P.T., work in Small Box Respirators and talk.	F K.
	10.45 - 11 a.m.	March to A Ground.	
	11 - 11.30 a.m.	Coy Drill.	A
	11.30 - 12.15 p.m.	Open Warfare Formation.	A
	12.15 - 1 p.m.	Bn.Drill and Demonstration.	A
	2 - 3 p.m.	Lewis Gun Instruction. Offs and Sergts.	
	3 - 5 p.m.	Recreational Training.	
WEDNESDAY. 24th.	8 - 8.30 a.m.	Inspections.	
	8.30 - 9.30 a.m.	2 Coys. Small exercise to bring in Open Warfare formations and action on meeting small points of resistance.	A
		2 Coys Drill, P.T., Musketry in Small Box Respirators and Talk.	A
	9.30 - 10.30 a.m.	2 Coys. Small exercise to bring in Open Warfare formations and action on meeting small points of resistance.	A
		2 Coys Drill, P.T., Musketry in Small Box Respirators and talk.	A
	10.30 - 11 a.m.	Battn. Drill.	
	11 - 12 noon.	2 Coys Assault Course and Musketry.	B
		1 Coy Rapid Wiring.	C
		1 Coy Patrolling.	D
	12 - 1 p.m.	2 Coys Assault Course and Musketry.	B
		1 Coy. Rapid Wiring.	C
		1 Coy. Patrolling and use of ground	
	2 - 3 p.m.	Lewis Gun Instruction. Offs and Sergts.	
	3 - 5 p.m.	Recreational Training.	
	5.30 p.m.	Lecture.	

2.

THURSDAY. 25th.		Scheme for cooperation with aircraft *and M.G. Bn.* / time and place to be arranged.	
FRIDAY. 26th.	8 – 8.30 a.m.	Inspections.	
	8.30 – 8.45 a.m.	March to Ranges.	
	8.45 – 9.45 a.m.	2 Coys. Musketry including Range Work.	E
		2 Coys. P.T., Work in Small Box Respirators and talk.	F K
	9.45 – 10.45 a.m.	2 Coys. Musketry including Range Work.	E
		2 Coys. P.T. Work in Small Box Respirators and Talk.	F K
	10.45 – 11 a.m.	March to A Ground.	
	11 – 12.15 p.m.	Attack Formations.	A
	12.15 – 1 p.m.	Bn Drill and Demonstration.	A
	2 – 3 p.m.	Lewis Gun Instruction. Offs and Sergts.	
	3 – 5 p.m.	Recreational Training.	
	8.30 p.m.	Lecture.	
SATURDAY. 27th.	8 – 8.30 a.m.	Inspections.	
	8.30 – 9.30 a.m.	2 Coys. Small exercise to bring in Open Warfare formations and action on meeting small points of resistance.	A
		2 Coys. Drill, P.T., Musketry in Small Box Respirators and talk.	A
	9.30 – 10.30 a.m.	2 Coys. Small exercise to bring in open Warfare formations and action on meeting small points of resistance.	A
		2 Coys Drill, P.T., Musketry in Small Box Respirators and talk.	A
	10.30 – 11 a.m.	Battn Drill.	
	11 – 12 noon.	2 Coys Assault Course and Musketry.	B
		1 Coy. Rapid Wiring.	C
		1 Coy. Patrolling and use of ground.	D
	12 – 1 p.m.	2 Coys. Assault Course and Musketry.	B
		1 Coy. Rapid Wiring.	C
		1 Coy. Patrolling and use of ground.	D
	2 – 3 p.m.	Lewis Gun Instruction. Offs and Sergts.	
	3 – 5 p.m.	Recreational Training.	

[signature] Capt. adjt.

Lieut. Colonel.
Comdg. 11th Bn. The SUFFOLK Regt.

19.7.18.

War Diary
11th Bn Suffolk Rgt (Camb)
August 1st – 31st 1918

WAR DIARY or INTELLIGENCE SUMMARY

Army Form C. 2118.

(Erase heading not required.)

Instructions regarding War Diaries and Intelligence Summaries are contained in F.S. Regs., Part II. and the Staff Manual respectively. Title pages will be prepared in manuscript.

Place	Date	Hour	Summary of Events and Information	Remarks and references to Appendices
LINGHEM	Aug 1st		Arrived in Lillers at 3.15 a.m. Day spent in resting.	
	Aug 2nd		Training continued.	
	Aug 3rd		Training continued. Demonstration to Battalion by H.Q. Demonstration Platoon.	Appendix I Appendix II
			Precautionary Defence Instruction issued.	
			Training Programme for ensuing week issued.	
	Aug 4th		Church Parade & Ceremonial. Inspection of Billets.	
	5		Training Continued.	
	6		Training Continued. Orders to LA LACQUE in Divisional Reserve by Route March. Training	Appendix III
			Party 5.30 p.m. Arrived in Lillers 7.30 p.m.	
LA LACQUE	7		Reconnaissance by C.O., Bombs of 10th Bde. line. Bn. moved to VALLORBA CAMP.	
			Lost draft arrived 7.30 p.m. Capln. Personnel left at LA LACQUE.	
	8	2 a.m.	Bn. moved to assembly point at Kroars. to form an advanced guard to the 61st	
LE SART SECTOR (Sheet 36A)		6.20 a.m.	Division. As soon as reports had been received that the enemy had withdrawn the line	
			the Bn. pursued over the top to get in touch with enemy going through the 12th R.War.Wicks.	
			LA By on right established a line approx. K33d.2 - K24d.77. CC1 + D By on left were line	
			opp. K24d.17 - K24a.15 - K20.5.6. LE SART FARM was occupied by our LP forced to retire to	
			close-ish fire from enemy pill boxes at/by numerous M.G.'s. An his twenty-tallied for 4 min. but no	
			reply was possible. the enemy then shelled this road. LP was not made hostile, No casualties arose by enemy	
			were patrolling By a.B Bty & L Bty Coys of 91 M.G. Bn had relieved B. C. Bty during the night	
			also 2 bn. R.G.H. relieved at midnight by LONTON HOUSE, Building on road, 147 of LONTON HOUSE	
VALLORBA CAMP	9		Bn also occupied posts at PIGEON FARM, LONTON HOUSE, Buildings on road, 147 of LONTON HOUSE	
	10		Arrived VALLORBA CAMP in Divisional Reserve. Rain until	Appendix IV
	11		Church Parade.	

WAR DIARY
or
INTELLIGENCE SUMMARY.
(Erase heading not required.)

Army Form C. 2118.

Place	Date	Hour	Summary of Events and Information	Remarks and references to Appendices
HALLOY CAMP	Aug 12		Training Continued	
	-13		Reconnaissance of Support line out Btn line by CO & Coy Cdrs. Training Cont'd. New Drafts 183rd Bde. relieved the 184 Bde. in the Corange sector. 11th Suffolks	
	-14		relieved the 7/8 O.B.L.I. & became Support Bn. Relief Rns. 7.30 pm.	Appendix V
FREMICOURT			Conflict to midnight	
	-15		Quiet – some harassing fire but settled on Support line	
PICQUET (Rest during)	-16		Quiet – normal activity	
	-17		ditto	
	-18		ditto	
	-19		Relieved 9th Northumberland Fusiliers in Right Front sector MARKERS G.E. Sects. Relief Complete by 1 a.m. 20th inst.	Appendix VI
	-20		Enemy pressing forward line – patrols following closely & found occupying Gaviches (1600 yds advance) Harassing fire. All incoming Patrols satisfied a further 1500* ahead. Only isolated patrols encountered. Bn. H.Q. moved forward to K.15.a.90.45. Heavy barrage on our new line 11.15pm–12.30am.	

Army Form C. 2118.

WAR DIARY
or
INTELLIGENCE SUMMARY.
(Erase heading not required.)

Instructions regarding War Diaries and Intelligence Summaries are contained in F. S. Regs., Part II. and the Staff Manual respectively. Title pages will be prepared in manuscript.

Place	Date	Hour	Summary of Events and Information	Remarks and references to Appendices
	Aug 28	10 am	Enemy opened in by arm on left to bring up here to left flank from Bde.	
	-29		Quiet. Remainder of Bn. relieved. The H/6 officers + 309 OR arrived. Dabagni Crop. Valuying.	
	-30		Quiet. Took small advance by Bn. on left. Valuying.	
	-31	9am	Quiet. Support Coys on Rout. March exercise. Dabagni. Ordered to "Stand by" ready. Enemy found.	
			Casualties during month.	
			Officers ORs	
			Killed — 11	
			Wounded 4 87	
			Wounded gas 7 223	
			Missing — 2	
			11 — 323	
			G.A. Tuck Lieut Col	
			Cmdg 11th Bn The Suffolk Regt	
			(Acting)	

SECRET.

Copy 13
Appendix I

11th Battalion THE SUFFOLK REGT.

DEFENCE INSTRUCTIONS No.1.

Reference Sheet 36.A.

1. The Battalion is in G.H.Q. Reserve and as such may be called upon :
    (a) To move from the XI Corps Area.
    (b) To act as XI Corps Reserve in the event of an attack.

2. In accordance with above the formation of Brigade Groups may be necessary, and will take place on receipt of the order "FORM BRIGADE GROUP".

3. In the event of the order Form Brigade Group being issued, the undermentioned will form the 183rd Infantry Brigade (LINGHAM BRIGADE) Group :

   183rd Infantry Brigade.
   No.3 Sec.61st Div.Sig.Coy.
   "B" Coy. 61st Bn.M.G.C.
   478 Field Coy. R.E.
   2/3rd Field Ambulance.
   No.3 Coy.61st Div.Train.

4. Major G.West will proceed to and report at Bde.H.Qs. FONTES for instructions.

5. The Battalion will be ready to move at short notice in Fighting Order.

6. Acknowledge.

                                            Lieut. and A/Adjutant,
2:8:18.   11th Battalion THE SUFFOLK REGIMENT.

        Copy No.1   C.O.
             2   Major G.West. ✓
             3   ..   J.H.Brett. ✓
             4 - 7   Companies. ✓
             8   Battn.H.Qs. ✓
             9   Q.M. ✓
            10   T.O. ✓
            11   R.S.M. ✓
            12 - 13 File. ✓
            14   183rd Brigade. ✓

Appendix I

SECRET.   11th Battalion The SUFFOLK Regiment.

DEFENCE INSTRUCTIONS No. 2.

Sheet 36.A.

1. In the event of the Battalion having to move from XI Corps Area the move will take place either :-
   (a) by March Route.
   (b) by Train.
   (c) by Bus.
   (d) by a combination of a, b and c.

In all cases of 1 (a) Route will be detailed when destination is known.

(b) In case of 1 (b) if move takes place by strategical trains, the whole of the Bde Group will move by rail. Probable entraining stations are ~~AIRE~~ or ~~HAZEBROUCK (3½ miles S. by N. of ST OMER.~~ BERGUETTE   ST OMER

(c) In case of 1 (a) probable embussing places are N.B9.c.7.0. - N.25.a.3.9. on the ST HILAIRE - ~~AUCHY AU BOIS ROAD.~~ AIRE ROAD

3. ACKNOWLEDGE.

Lieut & A/Adjutant.
11th Bn The SUFFOLK Regt.

Copy No. 1.   C.O.
        2.   Major Brett
        3.   West
      4 - 7.   Coys.
        8.   H.Qrs.
        9.   T.O.
       10.   Q.M.
       11.   R.S.M.
       12.   183rd Bde.
     13 - 14   File.

SECRET.   11th Bn The SUFFOLK Regt.

DEFENCE INSTRUCTIONS No.3.

Appendix I

Ref sheet 36 A. (The Div acting as XI Corps Reserve in case of
                                attack.)

1.   On the order "MAN BATTLE POSITIONS" the Bde plus B coy
      61st Bn M.G.Cy will be prepared to carry out :-
      (1) To extend the left flank of XI Corps from EBB GD DAM
           (K.B.a.4.0.) along the BOURRE RIVER and the BRAS DE AL BOURRE
           (K.B.a.-B.35.d. - D.34).
      (2) To extend the left flank of XI Corps from LA-MOTTE-AU Bois
           along the canal bank, running through D.18 and D.14.
      (3) To counter attack N.E. to drive the enemy back across
           the canal in D.18 and D.14.
2.   The Bde concentration area will be Area "L" STEENBECQUE-
      BOIS-BLARINGHEM-THIENNES.
3.   The move to this area will be by lorry in accordance with
      attached table. Coys marching independently to starting
      Point N.21.a.9.7. Debussing point head of column I.7.d.5.4.
4.   Lewis and Vickers Guns will be taken in the lorries.
5.   On arrival at STEENBECQUE A and B Coys will proceed as an
      advanced guard to undermentioned important tactical localities
      and relieve the nucleus garrisons of Cyclists and Corps Cavalry
      (KEH)
           A Coy to DENISE FARM locality J.2.c.
           B Coy to DELEGATE FARM   " J.1.b.
      Half section of 61st M.G.C. will proceed with both A and B Coys.
      and be under their Command.
      B Coy will on arrival establish touch with nucleus garrison
      of troops of 15th Corps about the level crossing in D.35 .
      A Coy will gain touch with a platoon of 11th Corps Cyclists
      at point where light railway passes through BOURRE-STEENBECQUE
      Line in J.14.c.
           The tasks of the above garrisons are :-
      (1) To collect and reform any troops falling back on their
          localities.

      (2) To act as guides to reinforcing troops.
      (3) In event of rapid enemy advance to create a block
           until such time as reinforced.
           They will be available to Move forward with the Bn for
      Offensive or other operations, forward.
      The Bn less   A and B Coys will bivouac in fields along
      road running between I.5.d.70.85 and I.10.a.30.70.)
6.   The Adjutant will report to Bde Report Centre I.3.b.6.1.
      as soon as the Bn arrives in concentration area.
7.   In the event of circumstances rendering it desirable BUSSES
      will be parked at LINGHEM for the night.
           Major J.H.Brett will superintend embussing of the Battn and
      will ensure that convoy properly parked each evening.
           One section of 61st M.G.C. will embus with the Battn.
           The Bn will embus and be ready to move at one hours notice.
~~8.   Surplus personnel will remain at LINGHEM.~~

9.(a) The Q.M. Stores and Transport not required for fighting will
      concentrate in fields along road N.26.b.8.7 - N.29.d..7)just
      N.of AIRE).
      (b) Nucleus personnel will proceed to vicinity of MALLE LE COMTE
      exact location will be reported to Staff Captain, 183 Bde.
      immediately on arrival. Staff Captain will be with Brigaded
      Transport mentioned above.
      (c) On receipt of orders to occupy forward positions the following
      only will go forward and form a "Forward Echelon" of transport :
           Pack Animals
           8 Tool Limbers.
           Cookers.
           Water Carts.
           4 L.Gun Limbers.

SECRET.   11th SUFFOLK ORDER No.38.   Copy No.........

Ref Sheet 36 A 1/40,000.   1.8.18.   Appendix I

1. The Battalion will move this evening to GUARBECQUE.
2. Starting Point. S.E.Corner of Battalion Camp. Time.5.15 p.m.
   Order of March : Bn.H.Qrs, Drums, A, B, C and D Coys.
   Dress. Marching Order. Caps will be worn. ROUTE.
   LA LACQUE Bridge, Canal Bank, Cross Roads. I.33.c.2.4., G.10.b and d.
   There will be an interval of 300 yds (3 minutes) between Coys. The usual halts will be observed.
3. All Lewis Guns, Camp Kettles, Baggage etc to be loaded or ready for loading by 4.15 p.m.
   Transport Officer will ensure that all above baggage is clear of the Camp by 4.45 p.m.
4. ACKNOWLEDGE.

                                          Captain & Adjutant.
                                          11th SUFFOLKS.

Copy No.1 and 2   Retained.
     3 - 6   Coys.
     7.   T.O.
     8.   Q.M.
     9.   H.Qrs.
     10.   R.S.M.

SECRET.

11th SUFFOLKS OPERATION ORDER
No. 34.

Appendix II
Copy No......

8.6.18.

1. The following personnel will be left out of the line for training purposes and will proceed by march route to the Divisional Reception Camp, GRECQUES (G.27.) tomorrow under the command of Major J.H.Bretts:-
    - 5 Officers.
    - 9 Instructors.
    - 24 O.Rs. to be trained as Signallers(A.Coy.4,B.5,C.9,D.6.)
    - 48 O.Rs. (12perCoy.) to be trained as Lewis Gunners.
    - 8 O.Rs. (2per Coy.) to be trained as Rifle Bombers.
    - 16 O.Rs. (4 per Coy.) to be trained in Musketry.
    - 2 Cooks.
    - 2 Sanitary duties.
    - 5 Officers Servants.
    - 1 Groom.

    C.Q.M.S. Flack, C.Coy. will act as Q.M.S. for above party.
    Each Coy. will send 1 Lewis Gun complete for training purposes.

2. Parade 6 p.m. on Field by Orderly Room.
    Dress - Fighting Order.

3. A Lorry will call at GUARBECQUE at 1.30 p.m. for Officers valises, Lewis Guns, Cooking Utensils (to be provided by Q.M.) and mens packs. Baggage to be stacked ready for loading by 1.30 p.m. on Field by Orderly Room.
    The Cook detailed by B.Coy. and Major Bretts' servant will proceed with this lorry.

4. An advance party under Capt.R.J.Coles has proceeded to CRECQUES today to arrange billetting accomodation.

5. ACKNOWLEDGE.

[signature]

Captain and A/Adjutant,
11th SUFFOLKS.

Copy Nos 1 & 2 Retained.
3 - 6 Companies.
7. Sig. Officer.
8. Major J.H.Bretts.
9. Quartermaster.
10. Transport Officer.
11. R.S.M.

TRAINING PROGRAMME.

Appendix II

Day	Time	Activity
SUNDAY.		Church Parade. Inspection of Billets etc.

MONDAY.
(a) Firing on 100 yards Range all day.
(b) Remainder: Coy. Drill, Musketry.
                  Open Warfare Exercises.
                  Rapid Wiring.
                  Work in Small Box Resp.
                  Talks, Physical Training.

TUESDAY.   Battalion scheme on Manoeuvre Area.
      5.15 p.m.   Lecture.

WEDNESDAY. 8 a.m.   Inspections.
      8.15 - 11.15 a.m.   As for Monday (b)
      11.15 a.m.   Battalion Drill.
      1.30 p.m.   Officers and N.C.Os L.Gun Instruction.
      2.30 - 3.30 p.m.   Trainig. Specialists.
                                 Remaindr : Rapid Wiring.
                                                    Patrolling.
      3.30 - 4.30 p.m.   Physical Training.

THURSDAY.   Battalion Route March.
                            LA COUTURE-ESTREE BLANCHE-LIETTRES.
      2.30 - 4.30 p.m.   Specialists Training.
                                 Remainder : Demonstration.
                                                        Musketry.

FRIDAY.   8 a.m.   Inspections.
      8.15 - 11 a.m.   As for Monday (b)
      11 a.m.   Battalion Drill.
      2.30 - 4.30 p.m.   Specialist Training.
                                 Remainder : Rapid Wiring.
                                                    Patrolling.
      5.15 p.m.   Lecture.

SATURDAY.   Battalion Route March.
                            LAMBRES - FONTES.
      2.30 - 4.30 p.m.   Specialist Training.
                                 Remainder : Musketry.
                                                     Intercommunication.

Lieut. and A/Adjutant,
11th Battn. THE SUFFOLK REGT.

3:8:18.

Appendix 1

SECRET.   11th SUFFOLKS ORDER No. 50.   Copy No. 1

Ref: Sheet 36A 1/40,000.   6.8.18.

1. The 61st Division is relieving the 5th Division in the LEFT sector of the X1 Corps Front.
2. 183rd Infantry Brigade will be in Divisional Reserve as from the night of 6/7th August.
3. (a) 11th Suffolks will relieve the 2/8th Worcesters at LA LACQUE on the night 6/7th and will proceed to that area by route march.
   (b) Permanent Q.M.Stores and Transport Lines will be established at TANNEY and occupy lines and billets vacated by a unit of the 13th Inf Bde. They will proceed direct there this evening.
4. Starting Point : Road Junction in N.20.d.4.4.
   Time :   5.20 p.m.
   Order of March :.   Drums, H.Qrs, D.C.B.A.
   100 yds between each Coy and between rear Coy and Transport, 25 yds between each 6 vehicles of Transport.
   The 2 L.G. Limbers will march with Coys.
   Not more than 2 men will follow any vehicle. The L.G.O. will arrange with the T.O. for Transport of A.A.Guns.
   Dress : Full Marching Order: Steel Helmets will be worn.
5. All baggage and Officers valises will be at Q.M.Stores ready to load at 4 p.m. Mess Kit will be stacked outside the Mess ready to load at 4.45 p.m.
6. A Billetting Party under 2nd Lt W.F.Bregden has already gone on ahead.
7. Billets will be ready for inspection at 5 p.m.
8. ACKNOWLEDGE.

                                        Lieut & A/Adjutant.
                                        11th Bn The SUFFOLK Regt.

        Copy No.1 and 2.   Retained.
               3 - 6.   Coys.
                  7.   T.O.
                  8.   Q.M.
                  9.   H.Qrs.
                 10.   L.G.O.
                 11.   R.S.M.
                 12.   183 Brigade. (For information.)

SECRET.   Copy No.
  11th Suffolk Order No 51. Appendix 1
Ref 36 ANE. 1/20,000.   9-8-18

1. The Battalion + details attached will
   be relieved tonight by 183 Bde.
   On completion of relief the Bn
   will proceed to VILLORBA CAMP (J.15.c)

2. B Coy will move at dusk to
   Bunkers at K.29.c.4.8. where B
   + C Coys H.G. Limbers will be loaded.
   B + C Coys less L.G Limbers will
   move to Camp via Southern Side
   of FOREST - CROIX MARCOUSSE
   A + D Coys will be relieved by
   2/8th Worcesters.
   Completion of relief to be reported
   by phone by code word "BOW"
   On relief A + D Coys will proceed
   to Camp via CURRA - CROIX MARCOUSSE,
   meeting L.G Limbers at FOREST.

3. All Coys will take out full
   complement of Rifle Ammunition,
   SA Bombs, Very Lights, S.O.S
   Signals, Wire Cutters, Flares,
   empty Petrol Tins and

Sermons:
All maps will be brought out, except Disposition Sketches.

4. Guides will be at entrance of camp to guide coys to huts.

5. As 2 Coys of Mortar Tacrs, will be achieved by MT transport as already detailed vanguard. On relief they will entrain at R.S.C. 11 after 4 hrs + proceed to ARCADE CAMP.
183 LMNB on relief by 182 LMNB will proceed to STEREMINO Camp.
2 Sections B Coy 61 MG Bn on relief by a Coy 61 MG Bn will rejoin 61 MG Bn.

6. ACKNOWLEDGE

E. D. Maton

Issued
7.45pm

Appendix V

SECRET.   Copy No... 12
                    11th SUFFOLKS Order No. 89.
Ref Sheet 28 A.   14.8.18.

1.   The 122nd Bde will relieve the 184th Bde in the AVERAGE SECTOR tonight.
     The 11th Suffolks will relieve the 2/4th O.B.L.I. and become Support Battn.
     Battn. H.Qrs. will be at K.8.c.35.85
                 "   "   " " K.8.c.90.15 (FRANK FARM)
     R.A.P.

2.   The Bn will proceed by platoons at 2 mins interval starting from entrance of camp at 7.30 p.m. in order C,D,A,B, Bn.H.Q. and will meet platoon guides at point where railway cross VIA ROMA.

3.   The following will leave O.R. at 4.30 p.m. under 2nd Lt.F.E. CATCHPOLE.
        1 N.C.O. per Coy and Bn.H.Qrs to take over stores.
        1 N.C.O. and 2 men, D Coy to relieve a guard at STATION EH.

4.   All defence schemes, maps, trench stores, petrol tins, etc to be taken over and signed for. Lists to be sent to O.R. by 8 a.m. tomorrow.
        Disposition sketches to be at O.R. at same time.

5.   Relief complete will be notified to Bn H.Qrs by the following code words.
        A Company.   DOG ABSENT.
        B   "   PAPER BURNT.
        C   "   CLOCK ORDER.
        D   "   SIZES DIFFERENT.

6.   The T.O. will arrange to convey Lewis Guns, Dixies, Rations, Trench Kits etc to K.8.c.3.8. to meet Coys and Bn.H.Q. Coys and Bn.H.Qrs will themselves take on their limbers as required.

7.   The T.O. will also arrange to convey all other stores and baggage to Q.M.Stores. This baggage will be stacked at Camp entrance by 4 p.m.

8.   ACKNOWLEDGE.

                                        S.J.Mason.
                                        Lieut & A/Adjutant.
                                        11th SUFFOLKS.

        Copy No.1 and 2   Retained.
             3 - 6   Coys.
               7.   T.O.
               8.   Q.M.
               9.   H.Qrs.
              10.   R.S.M.
              11. 2/4th   O.B.L.I.
              12.

Route: Along S. edge of forest to FOREST CORNER - VIA ROMA.

S E C R E T.   Copy No..1....

Appendix VI.

11th SUFFOLKS ORDER No. 85.   12:8:18.

Reference Sheet 36.A. N.E.

1. The Battalion will relieve the 9th N.F. in the Right Subsection of the ARREWAGE Sector tonight 12/13th inst. – 19th/20th
   B.Coy. will relieve A.Coy. 9th N.F. and become Right Front Coy.
   A. "   "   "   B. "   "   "   "   "   Left Front Coy.
   C. "   "   "   D. "   "   "   "   "   Right Support Coy.
   D. "   "   "   C. "   "   "   "   "   Left Support Coy.
   Battalion H.Qs. will be at K.8.c.2.2.
   No movement in connection with relief until dusk.

2. All Photos, Papers, Maps, and Trench Stores, and Work in hand will be taken over.
   List of Trench Stores taken over will be sent to Battn.H.Qs. by 8 a.m. 20th inst.

3. Advance Parties from the 9th N.F. will report at respective Coy.H.Qs. this afternoon.

4. Guides from the 9th N.F. will report as under:-
   for Right Front Coy.   1 per platoon and 1 per Coy.H.Q. at Trench and Road Junction K.15.a.05.45 at 7.45 p.m.
   1 per Post (eight) at K.15.d.75.35 at 8.30 p.m.
   for Left Front Coy.   1 per Platoon and 1 per Coy. H.Q. at A.Coy. H.Q. at 7.45 p.m.
   1 per Post (eight) on Road by SWINGBRIDGE (K.15.d) at 8.30 p.m.
   for Right Support Coy. 1 per Platoon and 1 per Coy. H.Q. on Road 100 yds. S.E. of HORSE SHOE DUMP (K.8.d.) at 7.45 p.m.
   for Left Support Coy. 1 per Platoon and 1 per Coy.H.Q. at D.Coy. H.Q. K.8.a.80.05 at 7.45 p.m.

5. Rations will come up cooked to MEREDITH STATION and then pushed to point where railway crosses canal for B.and C.Coys, and point where railway meets DENSEFARM Road for A. and D.coys.
   Water for B. and C.Coys is obtained from Water Point near Bn.H.Qs. and for A. and D.Coys from CHINESE FARM.
   C. and D.Coys. will find these pushing and carrying parties.

6. On relief the Guard at Bde.H.Qs. furnished by A.Coy., ~~the Guard at the Station will be furnished by B.Coy~~., and the two Signallers on the Power Buzzer Station will report to Right Bn.H.Qs. at K.8.c.2.2. for duty as Dump and Water Guards, etc. They will be rationed with Bn.H.Q.

7. Completion of relief will be notified to Battn.H.Qs. by the following codes:-
   A.Coy.   REAPING HOOKS REQUIRED.
   B. "   BILL HOOKS WANTED.
   C. "   CANNOT SAY.
   D. "   DO NOT REQUIRE ANY.

8. ACKNOWLEDGE.

Captain and Adjutant,
11th Battalion THE SUFFOLK REGT.

Copy No. 1   War Diary.
         2.   File.
         3 - 6 Companies.
         7.   Battn. H.Qs.
         8.   Intelligence Officer.
         9.   Quartermaster.
        10.   Transport Officer.
        11.   Medical Officer.
        12.   9th Bn. N.F.

SECRET.   Appendix VII   Copy No. 1.

11th SUFFOLKS ORDER No. 54.

20-8-18.

Ref. Sheet 36. A. N.E. 1/20,000.

1. (a) The Division is now on the general line K.36.b.0.5 - COLLEGE K.23.d.5.6 - thence along the Road running North to VIERHOUCK.
      Patrols are reported to be at GRAVE FARM - ATOM FARM - BRONCO FARM.
      The Division is in touch with 74th Division on the Right and 31st Division on the left.
   (b) The enemy is withdrawing, but it is uncertain to what position he has decided to retire.

2. The 74th Division has been ordered to advance & endeavour to reach the line of the River LAWE today.

3. 183rd Inf. Bde. has been detailed to act as Advanced Guard to the Division and for the purpose of this operation is composed as follows:-
      Commander: G.O.C. 183rd Inf. Bde.
      2 Batteries R.F.A.
      2 Sections 478 Field Coy. R.E.
      1 M.G. Coy. ("A" Coy. 61st Bn. M.G.C.)
      183rd Infantry Brigade.
      A portion of a Field Ambulance.

4. If the enemy is not encountered the Brigade will continue the forward movement, within the boundaries of the Division given in para 5 below, until touch with the enemy has been gained.

5. Boundaries of the Division are as follows:-
   Southern Boundary.   LYS CANAL
   Northern Boundary.   VIERHOUCK - COCHIN CORNER (exclusive) NEUF BERQUIN (15.a.0.0.) thence along Grid line due East.

6. (a) The 11th Suffolks plus 1 Sec. R.F.A., 1 Sec. "A" Coy. 61st Bn. M.G.C. and 1 Sec. 478 Field Coy. R.E. has been ordered to act as advance guard to the Brigade, and endeavour to establish itself on the general line LOUNGE HOUSE (L.32.b) - CHAPELLE DUELLE - TROMPEBRIDGE - RUE MONTIGNY (L.15.a)
   (b) The 11th Suffolks will operate within the boundaries given in para 5 and will as the first objective gain the line given in para 6 a.
   (c) The advance will be made as quickly as possible consistent with the maintenance of touch of the Coys. operating in the front line.
      The first bound will be the general line of the road running 250x S.W. of the Church in NEUF BERQUIN - SKELTER CROSS - CRINQUETTE LOTTIE. The second bound to the line of the objective.

7. D. Coy. will be on the Right & will keep touch with 74th Div. troops & will operate between the LYS CANAL and the line CARE CROSS thence along road running W. & E. through L.25.c & d - L.26. c & d inclusive.

- 2 -

C. Coy. will operate between the road running W & E. through L.25.c & d, L.26.c & d (exclusive) and the line GREVE FARM - SKELTER CROSS (inclusive). ~~B. Coy. will operate between the line GREVE FARM - SKELTER CROSS (inclusive) and grid line running W & E. through K.24 - A.L.19. + L.20 thence along track running W&E immediately N. of grid line running W&E through K.24, L.19 & track running W&E immediately N. of grid line through L.20 (exclusive) and to and will keep its left flank on~~ the line of PULLET FARM, - Road L.14.d.7.2. (inclusive) on which line its left flank, will rest.

Coys. will report at once when they are in assembly positions and will move forward at zero hour, to be notified by Bn. H.Q.

8. (a) Bn. H.Q. will be at K.15.a.9.5. with an advanced report centre at SACHET FARM (K.23.a.)
   Aid Post will be established in trench in K.15.d.

(b) Signal Officer will establish communication between Coys. and Bn. H.Qrs. by telephone where possible and visual.

~~9. 1st Bn. E. Lancs. Regt. plus 1 Sec. R.F.A. and 1 Sec. "A" Coy. 61st Bn. M.G.C. will act as left flank guard~~

(c) Light Signals with artillery are as follows:-

"A" For attack by enemy - present SOS, GREEN over GREEN over GREEN.

"B" Call for supporting fire - To lengthen range — RED Very Lights.

"C" To indicate position of our Infantry — WHITE Very Lights.

"D" Shorten Range - GREEN Very Lights.

9. 1st Bn. E. Lancs. Regt., plus 1 Sec. R.F.A. and 1 Sec. "A" Coy. 61st Bn. M.G.C. will act as left flank guard.

10. ACKNOWLEDGE.

W. Fanny

Captain & Adjutant.
11th SUFFOLK REGT.

SECRET. Appendix VIII. Copy No. 1.

11th SUFFOLKS ORDER No. 55

21-8-18

Ref. Sheet 36.A. N.E. 1/20000.

1. The 11th Suffolks will be relieved by the 9th N.F. and elements of the 1st Bn. E. Lancs. tonight 21/22nd inst.
   (a) 1st Bn. E. Lancs. will extend South & relieve A. Coy. & elements of B. Coy. as far as the track (exclusive) running immediately S. of the centre Grid Line in L.19.
   (b) 9th Bn. N.F. will relieve elements of B. Coy. and C. Coy. from Track below Centre Grid Line in L.19. (inclusive) to the LYS CANAL.
   (c) D. Coy. N.F. are already in position.

2. On relief the Bn. will withdraw to Bde. Reserve and be disposed as under:-
   A. & C. Coys. in K. 16. c & d.
   D. Coy. in K. 16. c.
   B. Coy. in K. 10. c. & d.
   Bn. H.Qrs. TANKARD FARM.

3. Guides as arranged.

4. Completion of relief and arrival in new area will be reported by code word "CERTAINLY"

5. The Section R.F.A., Section M.G.C., French Mortars and Section 478 Field Coy. R.E. will pass to Command of 9th N.F. on completion of relief.

6. ACKNOWLEDGE.

Laming.
Captain & Adjutant
11th SUFFOLK REGT.

11th SUFFOLKS ORDER No. 41.

Reference Sheet 36.A.

1. The 1st Bn. East Lancs. Regt. will relieve the Battalion in the Right Sub-sector on the night 30/1st July.
   On relief the Battalion will withdraw to HAMEL BILLET and be in Brigade Reserve.

2. Guides at the rate of 1 per Platoon will report to Battn. H.Qs. at HAMEL BILLET at 9.45 p.m. and guide Platoons to the Coy. H.Qs.
   These guides will be furnished by the Coy. in Reserve.
   Guides at the rate of 1 per Post will report to their respective Coy. H.Qs. at 11 p.m.

3. Completion of relief will be reported to Battn. H.Qs. by the following code words:-
   A. Company   ...   "AMMUNITION CORRECT."
   B.   "   ...   "BILL-HOOKS WANTED."
   C.   "   ...   "CORPORAL COMING."
   D.   "   ...   "DO YOU AGREE."

4. Arrival at HAMEL BILLET will be reported by Runner.

5. The Transport Officer will arrange for Limbers for Coy. and Bn. H.Qs. Mess Kit, Officers Trench Kit, Orderly Room Boxes and Cooks' Stores to be at Battalion H.Qs. at 10.30 p.m.

6. Lewis Guns will be carried out by Coys.

7. The Quartermaster will arrange to take over Billets, Stores, etc. Coys. will take over same Billets as before.

8. ACKNOWLEDGE.

Copy No. 1 & 2 Retained.   Captain and Adjutant,
        3 - 6 Companies. 11th Bn. THE SUFFOLK REGIMENT.
        7. Sig. Officer.
        8. Intelligence Officer.
        9. Quartermaster.
       10. Transport Officer.
       11. A/R.S.M.
       12. 1st E.Lancs.

SECRET.   **11th SUFFOLKS ORDER No. 43.**   Copy No........
Appendix TII
6:7:18.

1. The following inter-company reliefs will take place on the night 7/8th inst. :-
    A.Coy. will relieve D.Coy. and become Left Front Company.
    C. "   "   "   B. "   "   "   Right   "   "
    B.Coy. will be in Support.
    D. "   "   " " Reserve.
2. 1 N.C.O. per Platoon will be sent to their respective new areas on night 6/7th inst.
3. All Trench Stores will be handed over and work on hand etc. carefully explained.
4. Completion of relief will be notified to Battn.H.Qs. by the code words :-
    A.Coy.   "RATIONS AGREE"
    B. "   "RATIONS BAD"
    C. "   "CUT UP RATIONS"
    D. "   "RATIONS DIRECT"
5. Acknowledge.

Copy No. 1 & 2 Retained.
         3 - 6 Companies.
         7. Q.M. & T.O.
         8. I.O.& S.O.
         9. O.C.Right Bn.
        10.   "   478 Coy. R.E.
        11.   "   Left Group R.F.A.
        12.   "   M.G:Bn.

Captain and Adjutant,
11th Bn.THE SUFFOLK REGT.

SECRET.   Copy No. 1

              11th SUFFOLKS OPERATION ORDER   Appendix VI.
                         No. 37.   19.6.18.

Ref. Sheet 36.A.
1.   The personnel under training at the Divisional Reception Camp
N.20.d. (~~Mazure~~) will rejoin their Coys. on the 20th inst., with the
       following exceptions :-
                C.Q.M.S. Flack.
                2 Cooks.
                2 Sanitary men.
                48 O.Rs. under instruction in the Lewis Gun.
2.   On the 20th inst. the following personnel will proceed to the
       Divisional Reception Camp for further instruction :-
                1 Officer detailed by B.Coy. (and Servant)
                2 Officers detailed by C.Coy. (and Servants)
                2 Corporals.
                2 Lance Corporals } per Company.
                24 Privates.
                6 Signallers.
       Parade 2 p.m. outside the Orderly Room.
       Dress. - Marching Order, Steel Helmets will be worn.
       The Officer detailed by B.Coy. will be in charge of the party.
       One Limber will proceed with the above party to take Officers'
       Valises, Rations, etc..

                                                    [signature]
                                               Captain and Adjutant,
       Issued at 11.30 a.m.   11th Bn. THE SUFFOLK REGIMENT.

       Copy No. 1 & 2 War Diary & Retained.
                3 - 6 Companies.
                7. Battn. H.Q.
                8. Q.M.
                9. T.O.
                10. R.S.M.

Lorries are allotted as under :-

From head of column -
A.Coy. plus ½ Section B.Coy. 61st Bn.M.G.C. (1 Officer and 14 O.Rs.)
Numbers 1 - 7.

B.Coy. plus ½ Section B.Coy. 61st Bn.M.G.C. (1 Officer and 14 O.Rs.)
Numbers 8 - 14.

C.Coy. Numbers 15 - 20 and half No.21.

D.Coy. Half No.21 and Numbers 22 - 27.

B.H.Q. Numbers 28 - 32.

Lorry No.33 carries S.A.A.

Appendix IX

SECRET.   11th SUFFOLKS ORDER No.44.   Copy No........

Ref Map HAZEBROUCK S.A.   28.7.18.

1. The Battalion will proceed to the HERINGHEM-CAMPAGNE Area today by march route.
2. Starting Point - Fork roads North of M. in LINGHEM. Time 11 a.m. Order of march Drums, H.Qrs, D.B.C.A. 100 yds between each Coy. and between rear Coy and Transport, 25 yds between each 6 vehicles off transport. The 8 L.G.Limbers will proceed with Coys, the limber containing the A.A.Gun will have two men with it. Not more than two men will follow any vehicle.
   Dress: Marching Order, Steel Helmets will be worn.
3. All Training Stores will be taken to new area.
4. Officers Valises, Mess Kit etc will be stacked by Mess near Road ready to load by 10 a.m.
   All other baggage to be at Q.M.Stores by 9.30 a.m.
5. A billetting party under 2nd Lieut. F.B.Mothersole.M.M. has gone forward to new area. 2nd Lt F.B.Mothersole.M.M. will detail a guide from above party to meet the Bn at BOMMES CHURCH at 1.30 p.m.
6. One lorry will report to Q.M.Stores to assist in move. Q.M. will detail a guide to report to Bde H.Qrs at 1.45 p.m. to act as guide. When loaded this lorry will proceed direct to Cross Roads at BELLE CROIX. 2nd Lt.Mothersole will detail a guide to meet lorry at above cross roads at 2.30 p.m.
7. Dinners will be cooked on the cookers and will be served en route.
8. Sick Parade at 9.30 a.m.
9. Billets will be ready for inspection at 10.30 a.m.
10. ACKNOWLEDGE.

                                              Captain & Adjutant.
                                                 11th SUFFOLKS.

Issued at 7 a.m.

SECRET   Appendix IX   Copy No. 6

11th SUFFOLKS ORDER No. 56

23-8-18

Ref. Sheet 36. A. NE

1. The line now held by 183 Inf. Bde. is as follows:- L.31.b.00.60 — L.25.b.20.00 — Lily central — L.14.d.10.50 — L.14.b.30.30.

2. The 110th Inf. Bde. last night established the line COCHIN CORNER — PONTE RONDON.

3. (a) At 4 p.m. today 23rd Aug. 110th Inf. Bde. are advancing to the line BISHOPS CORNER — BECKET CORNER (F.26.) The Right Boundary of the advance of this Bde. is the line of the road L.15.b.2.70 — RUE PROVOST

(b) In conjunction with this advance by the Bde. on our Left, the 11th The Suffolks will advance and make good the following line which will be consolidated as soon as it has been reached — L.14.b.30.20 — along the road & track to L.9.d.65.00 — thence northward to BISHOPS CORNER where touch with the 110th Inf. Bde. will be established.

On our Left will be in conjunction with the Bde. on our Left. Line of the road COCHIN CORNER — NEPRON —

4. At the conclusion of the above operation the line held by the Bde. will be the line from the present boundary on our left to BISHOPS CORNER (F.26.)

5. The line held by the Bn. as the outcome of today's operations will be consolidated as follows:-
(a) A line of Lewis gun Posts will be established on the line L.31.b.00.60 — L.25.b.20.00 — Lily central — L.14.d.10.50 — along road & track to L.9.d.65.00 — N. to BISHOPS CORNER.
(b) A line of Resistance in rear of (a) on the following works — RUDERMATZ — TULLET FARM — RD.16.B — GOYT.B — CANE — 95.10 — BOWERY COTTAGES — Road junction L.L.b. 10.80 — RUE PROVOST and L.2.a.

2

The line in (4) above will be developed in the first place on the system of [...] and mutually supporting localities [...] about the points given. The linking up of these points is a matter for the future.

(c) O.C. Coys. in line will be responsible for touch and mutual support with the Coys. on their flanks.

6. The section of the Field Coy. at present attached to each Battn. will generally supervise the development of the field of [Resistance].

7. M. Guns will be disposed in the [line] of Resistance, and behind it, under arrangements made by O.C. M. Gun Bn.

8. Boundaries. Boundaries of the Bde. will be re-adjusted as follows:—
   Southern Boundary as at present.
   Northern Boundary — The [grid line K. H.] central — [...] central.
   Inter Battn. Boundary — The line KENNET FARM — ATEM FARM — PUHET FARM — HEMERAE [CHAIR] [...] [...] to Keyes [...]

9. The following re-adjustments of [...] will take place tonight 23/24th Aug.—
   (a) 9th North. Fus. will [relieve] Norfolks on the [...]
   (b) 11th Suffolks will relieve 1st [...] [...]
   (c) 1st [...] [...] of the Bde. front and will also the support [...]
   3 Coys. F.— BOYAR FARM
   [...] on the line VIERHOEK — PLATE BECQUE — NOTRE DAME [...]
   (d) Completion of relief [...] [...] [...] "HED FAST" [...]
   by the above hour.

10. [...] [...] [...] [...] [...] the move from the forward post forward in [...] [...] Coys.

11. ACKNOWLEDGE.

   W. Smith
   Capt. & Adjt.
   11th SUFFOLK REGT.

Appendix X

SECRET.   Copy No.
11th SUFFOLK ORDER No. 57.
                                         24.8.18.

1. At dusk tonight D. Coy will extend its area south to K.19. central inclusive & meet up the 9th Bn. N.F.
   A Coy. will lend D Coy any men required up to 30.

2. All arrangements to be made between A & D Coy. Commanders, and D Coy Commander and 9th N.F. Coy Commander.

3. Completion of relief to be reported to Bn. Hd. Qrs. the code words Boots required.

4. Acknowledge.

                    W Manning
                    Capt & Adjt
                    11th Suffolk R.

SECRET   Appendix X   Copy No.

11th SUFFOLKS ORDER No. 58.   24-8-18.

1. The 11th Suffolks will be relieved by the 2/1st Bn. 4 Bucks L.I. tonight 24/25 Aug.
        D. Coy. will be relieved by A. Coy. 2/1st Bucks L.I.
        C.   "   "   "   "   "   "   B.   "   "   "
        B.   "   "   "   "   "   "   C.   "   "   "
        A.   "   "   "   "   "   "   D.   "   "   "
   (with minor alterations as already arranged between Coy. Cmdrs.)

2. On relief B. & C. Coys. will take up a position in the Main Line of Resistance, A. & D. Coys. a position near Bn. Hqrs. at CHAPEL BOOM. Guides for the Coys. for the new area will be at present Bn. Hq. unless otherwise notified.

3. Each Coy. will send five guides to Bn. Hqs. by 6-15 p.m. for incoming Platoons & Coy. Hqs.

4. Coys. will report relief complete by the code word HALF RATIONS to the present Hq., & arrival in new area by code word "FULL STOP" to CHAPEL BOOM.

5. All S.O.S. Signals & Very Lights will be brought out. All Paper Maps & Trench Stores will be handed over. List of Stores handed over to be sent to CHAPEL BOOM by 10 am 25th inst.

6. Rations & Coy. Cooks will be waiting in the new area.

7. Disposition Sketches in new area to be forwarded by Coys. to CHAPEL BOOM by 10 am on 25th inst.

8. ACKNOWLEDGE.

                O. Manning.
                Captain & Adjutant
              11th SUFFOLK REGIMENT.

SECRET.   Appendix "A"
Ref. Sheet.57.Ed.R. 1/40,000   *Appendix X*

1. Pending the issue of more detailed instructions the following
    moves will take place on ("A") the order "MAN BATTLE STATIONS"
    and ("B") the order to "OCCUPY POSITIONS".

                                    "A"

1. On the order "MAN BATTLE STATIONS" the Battn will move to
    assembly positions in Assembly Area "B" (Map T.S. ——) Field
    V.8.C.40.00. First Line Transport will accompany the Battn.
2. Brigade H.Q. in "B" assembly area will be established at
    T.C.5.75.00 where Capt. C.V.Canning.M.C. will report as soon
    as the Battn has arrived at the positions in (1) above.
3. The Battn will march further westward via Route "A" (Map T.S. 308)
4. Surplus personnel will remain behind in the present billets
    and await further instructions.

                                    "B"

1. On the order "OCCUPY POSITIONS" the Battn will move from
    Assembly Area "B" and occupy positions in the Army Line.
    from trench and Road Junction C.30.d.86.21. (inclusive) to Corps
    Boundary at P.31.c.30.90.
2. ACKNOWLEDGE.
                                                    C.V.Canning
    24.7.18.   Captain & Adjutant.
                                                    11th Bn The SUFFOLK Regt

Copies to Coys., T.O.,Q.M.,M.Gre, R.S.M.

11th Battalion THE SUFFOLK REGT.

PROGRAMME OF WORK.

Appendix XI

SUNDAY.		Church Parade. Ceremonial. Inspection of Billets. Baths.
MONDAY.	8 a.m.	Inspections and March to Training Ground followed by "The Drill of a Bn. Attack." Officers and Sergts. L. Gun Instruction.
	1.30 p.m. 3.30 p.m. – 4.30 p.m.	(Musketry, P.T., Small Box Respirator (drill, Rapid Wiring (Specialist Training under Specialist (Officers.
	5.15 p.m.	Lecture.
TUESDAY	Afternoon.	Battn Scheme. (Coy. Drill, Box Respirator Test (with Gas Chamber.
WEDNESDAY.	8 a.m.	Inspections and march to training Ground followed by "Wood Fighting" by Companies.
	2 p.m. 3.30 – 4.30 p.m.	Tactical Scheme for Officers. Bn Drill under R.S.M. followed by Musketry, P.T. and Small Box Respirator Drill.
THURSDAY. August Day MINDEN DAY	9 a.m.	Ceremonial Parade. Followed by work on "Y" Range.
FRIDAY.	Afternoon.	Battn Scheme. Patrolling Demonstration, specialist training under specialist Officers.
	5.15 p.m.	Lecture.
SATURDAY.	8 a.m.	Inspections and march to training ground followed by Bn Drill. Officers and Sgts. L.G. Instruction.
	1.30 p.m. 3.30 p.m. – 4.30 p.m.	(Musketry, P.T., Small Box Respirator (Drill and Rapid Wiring. (Specialist training under Specialist (Officers.

26.7.18.

for Lieut. Colonel.
Comdg. 11th Bn The SUFFOLK Regiment.

Appendix XII
Copy No......

SECRET.

11th Battalion THE SUFFOLK REGT.

DEFENCE INSTRUCTIONS.

Reference Maps, Sheet 27.Ed.3, 1/40,000.
Sheet 27.S.E., 1/80,000.

The Battalion now forms part of the XV Corps, IInd Army, and is temporarily held in G.H.Q. Reserve.

" A "

1. The Battalion must be prepared to move in Fighting Order at 3 hours notice.
   On receipt of the order "MAN BATTLE STATIONS" (followed by time) the Battalion will parade in Field at S.30.b.3.4 and will move to Assembly Positions by Route "A" in Field at V.8.c.4.0.
   100 yards interval will be maintained between Companies.
   First Line Transport, plus Mess Cart, will accompany the Battalion.
   The time given after the code words "MAN BATTLE POSITIONS" will be the time of parade on Field S.30.b.3.4.

2. Brigade H.Q. in the assembly area will be established at V.8.a.75.90, where the Adjutant will report as soon as the Battalion is in position.

3. Surplus personnel will assemble in 'B' Company Billet.

4. Acknowledge.

                                    Captain and Adjutant,
                              11th Battalion THE SUFFOLK REGT.

Copy No. 1 & 2 Retained.
         3 - 6 Companies.
           7   Officer i/c Battn.H.Q.
           8   R.S.M.
           9   Q.M.
          10.   T.O.

APPENDIX XII

SECRET.   Copy No. 1
                11th SUFFOLKS ORDER No.49.
Ref Sheet 36 A.   31.7.18.

1.   The Battalion will proceed to LINGHEM today by route march.
2.   Starting Point.:   Cross Roads in A.5.d.
     Time. :   9.35 p.m.
     Order of March.   Drums, H.Qrs, A.B.C. and D Coy.
     100 yards between each Coy and between rear Coy and Transport.
     25 yards between each 6 vehicles of transport. Not more
     than 9 men to follow any vehicle.
         The L.G.O. will arrange with the T.O. for carriage of A.A.
     Guns.   Dress: Battle Order with Haversacks instead of Packs,
     Steel Helmets will be worn.
3.   Training Stores will be taken.
4.   Packs will be stacked as arranged by Q.M.   Officers valises
     and other baggage will be stacked at Coy and Bn.H.Qrs by
     7.30 p.m. Mess Kit to be at Coy and Bn.H.Qrs at 8.15 p.m.
5.   A billetting party of 1 N.C.O. per Coy under Sec-Lt.W.F.
     Brogden will meet a lorry at Cross Roads at BELLE CROIX at
     3.15 p.m.
6.   All area stores will be handed over to Sub-Area Commandant.
7.   HOT DRINK will be cooked on cookers and served on arrival
     in billets.
8.   Special Sick Parade for those unable to march at 5 p.m.
9.   All billets to be ready for inspection at 8.30 p.m.
10. ACKNOWLEDGE.

                                       Lieut & A/Adjutant.
                                       11th Bn The SUFFOLK REGT

     Copy No.1 and 2.   Retained.
           3 - 6   Coys.
             7.   T.O.
             8.   Q.M.
             9.   H.Qrs.
            10.   L.G.O.
            11.   M.O.
            12.   R.S.M.

- 2 -

   (d)   32 Lewis Gun Drums per Gun will be taken into action - the remaining 12 drums will form a Battalion Reserve at Q.M. Stores.
2. A.A. Lewis Guns will be mounted at Transport Lines.
   (e)   All moves of Transport and Q.M. Stores will be notified to Bde. H.Qrs. and Supply Officer.
9. Tents and Trench Shelters will be struck and handed to 74th Divisional Reception Camp, and receipts obtained.
10. Q.M. will detail 4 Orderlies (mounted and cyclists) to remain with Q.M. Stores and Transport whose duty will be to keep touch and notify any change of situation. He will also detail one man to report daily to O.C. No.3 Coy. Div. Train to act as guide to supply wagons.

Lieut. TOULMIN will act as Liason Officer between Battalion H.Q. and Q.M. Stores and Transport.

2. Acknowledge.

J. Mason
Lieut. and A/Adjutant,
11th Battalion THE SUFFOLK REGT.

Copy No. 1.   C.O.
       2.   Major G. West.
       3.   " J.H. Brett.
     4 - 7   Companies.
       8.   Battn. H.Qs.
       9.   T.O.
     10.   Q.M.
     11.   R.S.M.
     12.   183rd Brigade.
   13 - 14 File.

Lorries are allotted as under :-

From head of column -

A.Coy. plus ½ Section B.Coy. 61st Bn.M.G.C. (1 Officer and 14 O.Rs.) Numbers 1 - 7.

B.Coy. plus ½ Section B.Coy. 61st Bn.M.G.C. (1 Officer and 14 O.Rs.) Numbers 8 - 14.

C.Coy. Numbers 15 - 20 and half No.21.

D.Coy. Half No.21 and Numbers 22 - 27.

B.H.Q. Numbers 28 - 32.

Lorry No.33 carries S.A.A.

WAR DIARY
or
INTELLIGENCE SUMMARY.

Army Form C. 2118.

Vol 33

War Diary
11th (S) Bn the Suffolk Regt (Cambs)
September 1st – 30th 1918

Army Form C. 2118.

WAR DIARY
or
INTELLIGENCE SUMMARY.
(Erase heading not required.)

Instructions regarding War Diaries and Intelligence Summaries are contained in F. S. Regs., Part II. and the Staff Manual respectively. Title pages will be prepared in manuscript.

Place	Date	Hour	Summary of Events and Information	Remarks and references to Appendices
Sheet	Sept 2nd	5.45	2/7 Bn. R. Scot. Regt. passed Rough lines & took up position	Appendix I.
B.G.N.E.			Main line of Defences on line - Loch in corner - POULET FARM	
CRINGWICK		10.7.15	Bn. to Kinawa to VILLORBA CAMP in	
SECTOR.			2nd Reserve. all in camp at 8pm.	
VILLORBA CAMP.			Cleaning up & refitting. 3 hours drill & 1 hour route march exercises	
	-3rd		Route March exercises & attack practices. Inspection of draft by B.G.C. 183 Inf. Bde. Lecture by A.P.M. 61st Divn.	
	-4th		Route Marches and attack practices: Musketry & Box Respirator drill.	
			Moved by light Rly. & March Route to Lt. Col. Montigny	Appendix II.
Rue Montigny	5th		A.E.F.A. Arrived 1.30 p.m. Bivouaced for night	
COBALT	-6th		Moved by March Route to SELSY FARM - COBALT COTTAGES	Appendix III.
COTTAGES			A.E.F.A. Arrived 11.30 a.m. Bivouaced for night.	
			Reconnaissance of front line of advance.	
	-7th		Ordered to relieve 2/7 R. Star Regt. (182 Bde) as advanced	

Army Form C. 2118.

WAR DIARY
or
INTELLIGENCE SUMMARY.
(Erase heading not required.)

Instructions regarding War Diaries and Intelligence Summaries are contained in F. S. Regs., Part II. and the Staff Manual respectively. Title pages will be prepared in manuscript.

Place	Date	Hour	Summary of Events and Information	Remarks and references to Appendices
Sheet 36.N.W.			Guard. Relief completed by 1 a.m.	Appendix
6.23.a.9.4.			Heavy shelling of Bridges & SAILLY-SUR-LYS (HE & Gas)	IV.
		8 p.m.-3 a.m.		
6.18.a.15.15 Sept.			Quiet. H.Q. moved to SAILLY-SUR-LYS at 6.18.a.15.15. Patrols active.	
		9—	C. Coy. advanced line, but forced to withdraw owing to heavy M.G. fire.	
	9/10		A Coy advanced left flank to establish at FROWINGHEM.	
		4 — 3 a.m.	D " advanced on FROWINGHEM though A Coy but forced to retire by sudden member. This attempt renewed	
		2 a.m.	at 3 a.m. and two new posts established 200+ in advance of general line.	
		11 a.m.	Relieved by 2/5 Bn GLOUCESTER REGT (184 Bde) to withdraw to ESTAIRES AREA in support. All filled at 3 a.m.	Appendix T
L.28.c.9.9	12—		Cleaning up, encountering Corps Battle line.	
	3—		Training. Superinent of hills. Tactical scheme under B.C. 183. T.B. H.Q. Commanding officers & Coy Commanders	

WAR DIARY
or
INTELLIGENCE SUMMARY.
(Erase heading not required.)

Army Form C. 2118.

Place	Date	Hour	Summary of Events and Information	Remarks and references to Appendices
L.28.t.95.	14 Sept		Training. Improvement of Fields, School schemes, Musketry Co.	
	15th		House Serve Baths. Work on billets.	
	16 -		Training continued, work on billets.	
	17 -		do.	
	18 -		Training (Coy attacks) in co-operation with M.G. Coy. and T.M.) Work on billets continued.	
	19 -		Route Marching exercise. Lewis Gunners, Trowers & Stretcher Bearers fitted with new Tripler eye pieces to Respirators.	
	20 -		Bn. Schemes in co-operation with M.G.C. and T.M.B. (Exhibition and Connection exercise)	
C.20.d.8.2.1.	21 -		Relieved 2/6 R. War. Regt. as Support Bn. of Advanced Guard Arrival VI Bde. H.Q. at G.20.J.m.8 (About 36mm). Relief completed by 10 p.	
	22 -		Quiet night. Work on defences, &c. Courses in Lewis Gun & Musketry.	
	23 -		Some air activity up to day = one Jerry Observator machine.	

Army Form C. 2118.

WAR DIARY
or
INTELLIGENCE SUMMARY.
(Erase heading not required.)

Instructions regarding War Diaries and Intelligence Summaries are contained in F. S. Regs., Part II. and the Staff Manual respectively. Title pages will be prepared in manuscript.

Place	Date	Hour	Summary of Events and Information	Remarks and references to Appendices
	24 Sep		occu. to Front line. Increased shelling at night.	
			General enemy casualties over – howze shift.	
			Gas discharge on Junction Fm & BARTLETTS POST at 11.5 p.m.	Appendix VII
	25		Gas discharge and attack on above posts performed to	VIII
			Quiet night.	
	26		Action in case of Enemy withdrawal ordered. Attack on Tuscan	Appendix IX
			POST & BARTLETTS FM. 10.10 p.m. Stretches gained wk & prisoners	
			+ M.G. but counter attack ejected us from posns.	
	27		Quiet day.	
	28		Relieved by 12/8 KRRC Regt. withdrawn to support Bde.	Appendix X
			(Corps Batt. line) Relief complete by 9 pm. All in	
			billets 11 p.m.	
L28.Q.99. 29.			Men to be paid.	
30.			Cleaning up. Inspection of Company's by CO.	
				Officers
				Killed, died of wounds, wounded.
			Casualties during month –	Other ranks
				— 1 —
				— 2.
				— 5. 38.

WAR DIARY or INTELLIGENCE SUMMARY

Army Form C. 2118.

Honours during work:-

MILITARY CROSS.   Capt. G.F.R. BAGULEY.
D.C.M.   43402 Cpl. N.H. EDWARDS, atta. Bn. HQ
Military Medal.   318898 Sgt. A.J. RASH
                  23634 Sgt. D.C. KNIGHTS
                  16600 Cpl. C. MABBUTT.
                  45067 Pte. E. WATKINS.

30.9.18.

G.I. Rush
Lt Col
C'm'dg. 11th Bn. Suffolk Regt.

SECRET.   11th SUFFOLKS Order No. 58. Copy No...... *Appendix*
                                              31.8.18.   *T.*
Ref Sheet 56 A. 1/40000
1.   The 11th Suffolks will be relieved by the 2/7th Warwicks in
the Main Line of Retention on 1st Sept.
     March Route On completion of relief, the Bn will withdraw to VILLORBA CAMP *by*
~~by Light Railway~~ and be in Divisional Reserve.
2.   S.O.S. Rockets, Very Lights and Trench Shelters will be brought
out. All other trench stores, paper maps etc will be handed over.
Receipted Lists of stores handed over to be sent to O.R. by
9 a.m. on 2nd Sept.
3.   Guides at the rate of 1 per platoon, 1 per Coy H.Q. and 1 per
Bn H.Q. will report to Lt.S.J.Mason at MEREDITH STATION at 2.15
p.m. 1st inst.
4.   As relieved Coys and Bn.H.Qrs will rendezvous at MEREDITH
STATION, ~~and report to Lt.S.J.Mason who will superintend entraining~~.
5.   All movement East of the Forest will be by platoons.
6.   Completion of relief will be reported to Bn.H.Q. by the code
word "DIRTY".
7.   Transport Lines and Q.M.Stores will not move. Rations and
Forage will be delivered to DUNCAN STATION.
8.   1 N.C.O. per Coy & Bn.H.Q. and a runner will report to Major.
J.H.Brett at 8.45 a.m. and proceed as billetting party.
9.   Transport Officer will arrange for one limber per Coy and one
limber for Bn.H.Qrs to report to the respective H.Q. at 2.30 p.m
to convey Lewis Guns, Mess and Cooks Kit etc to VILLORBA CAMP.
10.   ACKNOWLEDGE.
                                          A.Kenno
                                          Capt & Adjutant.
                                          11th Bn The SUFFOLK Regt.

        Copies No.1 and 2.   Retained.
               3 - 6   Coys.
               7 & 8   T.O. & Q.M.
               9 & 10.   H.Qrs & R.S.M.
               11 & 12.   2/6th R.Warwicks & 183 Brigade.

Appendix II.

SECRET.   11th SUFFOLKS ORDER No. 59.   Copy No...1

Ref. Sheet 36 A.   4.9.18.

1. The 11th Suffolks will move to the RUE MONTIGNY area tomorrow 5th inst.

2. Companies will parade at 9.40 a.m. and march to CROWE STN where they will report to the Adjutant.

3. The Battalion will detrain at LES PURESBECQUES, and proceed by march route via road junction K.29.b.05.50.-ROBERMETZ-NEUF BERQUIN. 100 yds distance will be maintained between Coys. Dress: Marching Order.

4. All stores and Kit as detailed to Coy Comdrs, to go forward will be stacked ready to load by the cookers at 8 a.m. All kit etc to be returned to Q.M. Stores will be stacked seperately by the cookers ready to load at 8 a.m. A Coy will detail a N.C.O. and C Coy one man to take charge of the latter kit. They will report at 7.30 a.m. to Sgt J.Ayres who will take charge of all stores and will report to Q.M. on arrival.

5. One N.C.O. per Coy and 1 for Bn.H.Qrs will report to Sec-Lt F.E. Catchpole at O.R. at 8.15 a.m. and proceed on bicycles as billetting party.

6. Bn.H.Qrs will be at L.13.b.2.8. Arrival of Coys will be reported by runner.

Capt & Adjutant.
11th Suffolks.

Copy No.1 and 2.   Retained.
       3 - 6   Coys.
       7 - 8   T.O. & Q.M.
       8 - 9   H.Qrs & R.S.M.
         10   183rd Brigade.

Appendix III.

SECRET.

11th SUFFOLKS ORDER NO. 80.

Copy No.......

5:5:18.

Ref. Sheet 36.A., N.E.

1. The 11th Suffolks will move to the SELSEY FARM – COBALT COTTAGES Area tomorrow 6th inst.
2. All French Shelters, Tents, etc. will be taken forward by Coys. One limber er Coy., and one limber and Mess Cart for Battn. H.Qs., will report at respective H.Qs. at 10.15 a.m.
3. 2/Lieut. Catchpole with 1 N.C.O. and 4 Runners of Battn. H.Qs. will go forward and take over Billets.
4. Coys. will move independently, moving off at 10.30 a.m., to Road junction at L.10.c.9.1., where guides will be met.
5. The Battalion will go into the line on the night 7/8th inst..
6. Coy. Cmdrs. will meet Major J.H.Brett at RUE MONTIGNY at 9.30 am. 6th inst to reconnoitre.
7. Coys. will report arrival in new area, and location of their H.Qs. by runner immediately on arrival.

Copy No. 1 & 2 Retained
       3 – 6 Coys.
       7. Battn.H.Qs.
       8 – 9 Q.M.& T.O.
      10. R.S.M.
      11 183rd Bde H.Qs.

Captain and Adjutant,
11th Battalion THE SUFFOLK REGT.

Appendix IV.

SECRET.   Copy No....1....

11th SUFFOLKS ORDER No.61.   7:V:18.

Ref. Sheet 36.A., N.E.
            36.N.W.

1. The 11th Suffolks will relieve the 2/7th Bn. Royal Warwick Regt. on the left of the advanced guard area tonight 7th inst.-
        A.Coy. will be Left Front Coy.
        C. "   " " Right "   "
        B. "   " " Left Support Coy.
        D. "   " " Right "   "
    Battn. H.Qs. will be at G.33.a.8.4.,
    Aid Post   "   "   on main road G.17.c.35.50.

2. 2/Lieut. F.S.Catchpole, with Runners and Signallers will proceed as Advance Party and reconnoitre all Coy. positions and keep in touch with the situation.

3. Coys. will send a sketch of their dispositions, and receipted lists of stores taken over to Battn. H.Qs. by 8 a.m., 8th inst.

4. 2/Lieut. J.D.Davis will be attached for duty to the Regt.Aid Post and will report to Commanding Officer forthwith.

5. Guides (1 per platoon and 1 per Coy.H.Qs.) will be met at the ROMM Pontoon Bridge near ROUGE MAISON POST at 8 p.m.
    Order of March - A. C. B. D.Coys Bn. H.Qs.

6. Transport Officer will arrange for one limber per Coy. and one per Battn. H.Qs. to report to respective H.Qs. at 5.30. p.m. to convey Lewis Guns etc., and to collect Officers valises, Haversacks, Cooks' Kit, etc. from respective H.Qs. for conveyance to Q.M.Stores.

7. Rations for the 8th inst will be carried on the men.

8. Relief complete will be reported to Battn. H.Qs. by the code word "WHERE".

9. ACKNOWLEDGE.

                                           Captain and Adjutant,
                                        11th Battalion THE SUFFOLK REGT.

Copy No. 1 & 2 Retained.
         3 - 6 Companies.
         7. Battn. H.Qs.
         8. Quartermaster.
         9. Transport Officer.
        10. R.S.M.
        11. 183rd Inf. Bde.

SECRET
Appendix V/4
Copy No. 1

11TH SUFFOLKS. ORDER No. 69.
11-9-18.

Ref. Sheet 36A N.W. & 36. N.W.

1. The Battn. will be relieved by the 2/5th Gloucesters tonight and on relief will proceed by Platoons at 100 yards intervals to bivouac just W. of ESTAIRES.

2. 5 Guides per Coy. to bring in relieving troops will report at Battn. H.Q. at 7 p.m.

3. Very Lights will be brought out, all other Trench Stores will be handed over and receipts taken and sent to Bn. HQ. by 10 a.m. 12th inst.

4. The T.O. will arrange to send the necessary Transport to fetch away L. Guns French baggage etc. L. Gun Limbers will meet Coys on Main ESTAIRES – ERQUINGHEM Rd.

5. Major G. Wise & the Q.M. will arrange to take over area at present occupied by 2/5th Gloucesters, prepare a hot meal on arrival, & send guides to meet Coys & Bn. HQ at L.29.d.H.Q.

6. The T.O. will arrange to bring Ration waters to this new area.

7. Completion of relief will be reported to Bn. HQ. by the Code word "ROMPU".

8. Coys. will also report arrival in new area.

9. ACKNOWLEDGE.

L. Latchbole Lieut. & Adjt.
Issued at 3 p.m.   11th SUFFOLKS.

Appendix VI.

SECRET.   11th SUFFOLKS ORDER No. 63.   Copy No.....

Ref: 36 A.N.E.   21.9.18.
     36 N.W.

1. The 11th SUFFOLKS will relieve the 2/6th R.Warwicks in Support position of Advanced Guard Brigade on the night of 21/22 Sept.
2. A Coy will relieve D Coy R.Warwicks.
    B "   "   " C "   "
    C "   "   " A "   "
    D "   "   " B "   "
3. Order of March : C.D.B.A. Coys. Bn.H.Qrs. 100 yds distance between platoons.   C Coy will move off at 7 p.m.
3. An Advance Party of 1 Officer per Company, 1 N.C.O. per platoon, 1 Officer, 1 N.C.O, 2 Signallers and 2 Runners per Bn. H.Qrs will report to Bn.H.Qrs at 2.15 p.m. and proceed to G.20.b. 4.2. and take over stores etc.
4. Trench Shelters at present on charge will be handed over on relief, except those in use at Q.M. Stores and Transport. Receipts will be forwarded to O.R. by 8 a.m. 22nd inst.
    Very Lights will be taken in the line.
    All S.O.S. Grenades, Flares, Tools, Reserve S.A.A. etc, will be taken over. List of Trench Stores taken over signed and countersigned to be sent to Bn.H.Q. by 8 a.m. 22nd inst.
5. Disposition Sketches of Companies will be sent to Bn.H. Qrs by 8 a.m. 22nd inst.
    Bn.H.Qrs will be at G.20.b. 4.2.
6. Guides at the rate of 5 per Company will meet Companies as under:-
    For C and B Coys at G.22.c.15.15.
     "   D " A "   " G.21.a.0.0
7. Kit for Q.M.Stores will be stacked by Companies at the Guard Room and at the Officers Mess Ready to load by 2.30 p.m.
    Lewis Guns and Kit for the Line will be stacked as above ready to load by 6.p.m.
8. ACKNOWLEDGE.

                                            Captain and Adjutant.
                                              11th SUFFOLKS.

    Copy No.1 and 2.   Retained.
         3 - 6.   Coys.
           7.   T.O.
           8.   Q.M.
           9.   H.Qrs.
          10.   R.S.M.
          11.   2/6th R.Warwicks.
          12.   183rd Brigade. (For Information).

Extract from Bde Order No 208
dated 24/9/18   Appendix VII

SECRET.

1. Tonight 24/25 inst (if wind is favourable) there will be a gas projector discharge against :-
   (a) JUNCTION POST area - H.32.a.8.3.
   (b) BARTLETTS FARM area- H.26.a.4.4.
   The night of the discharge will be known as "Y" night.

2. On "Y" plus 1 night there will be a projector discharge of smoke and innocuous Gas at the same targets in conjunction with which an attempt will be made to occupy Junction Post and Bartletts Farm.

3. The operation against the above enemy strong points will be carried out by Fighting Patrols of 1st EAST LANCASHIRE REGIMENT, and will be assisted by Artillery, Trench Mortar and Machine Gun fire.

4. The following codes will be used in connection with the discharge of gas:-
   "OPERATION WILL TAKE PLACE" ?............RHODE
   "OPERATION POSTPONED"   ISLAND
   "OPERATION COMPLETE"   RED
   "OPERATION CANCELLED"   HEN BOUND.
   Zero hour for the discharge of projectors will be communicated by giving the hour in figures as follows:-
      10.15 p.m. will be 1015.
      12.00 (midnight) will be 1200.
      1.45 a.m. will be 145.
   If the discharge is to take place at 1.45 a.m. message will read "145 RHODE".

5. Protective barrage round Junction Post and Bartletts Farm will be called for by a Rifle Grenade bursting into RED over GREEN over YELLOW
   (S.O.S. Signal for the remainder of the Brigade front remains unchanged).

24.9.18.   Capt and Adjutant.

SECRET.   Copy No ...2...

24.9.18.

11th SUFFOLKS ORDER NO 64.

RE. BRIGADE ORDER NO 248 dated 22.9.18.

1. In the event of the capture of BARTLETTS FARM and JUNCTION POST, the Officers Commanding the Garrisons of these posts will fire White Very Lights in quick succession should they require reinforcements to resist counter-attack.

2. O.C. 1st Bn.E.Lancs.Regt will arrange to hold 2 Platoons in readiness in rear of our outpost line W.of BARTLETT FARM and JUNCTION POST ready to at once reinfornce these localities if the signal is given.

3. In the event of these reinforcing Platoons being utilised, "B" Company of 11th Suffolks (now in G.23.a. and c) will hold themselves in readiness to occupy the area now held by the left Company of the right Battalion in the <u>outpost line of resistance</u>. The necessary reconnaissances will be made forthwith.

4. "A". Company 11th Suffolks W of the LYS Canal will in this case be ready to take the place of "B" Company now in G.23.a and c.

5. The order for move of Companies as above will be conveyed by code word "ANTHONY"

6. ACKNOWLEDGE.

Captain and Adjutant.
11th Battalion.The SUFFOLK Regt.

Issued at ....

Copy No 1.File.
2.War Diary.
3-6. Companies .
7. Bn.Hdqrs.
8. T.O.
9. Q.M.
10. 183rd Inf.Brigade.

Appendix IX

SECRET. COPY NO. 14
26.2.16.

11th BATTALION. The SUFFOLK REGIMENT.

ORDER NO 65.

ACTION IN CASE OF WITHDRAWAL of THE ENEMY

REF:- Sheet 36 A.N.W.

1. In the event of the retirement of the enemy from his present position the Advance Guard Brigade will make for the following objective:-
    Road Junction H.33.d.40.10 - CROIX BLANCHE - FLEURBAIX - ERQUINGHEM at point H.4.d.9.7.

2. The 11th Suffolk Regiment will be ready on receipt of orders to move to the present outpost line of resistance, taking over the present disposition of Companies in Support.
    "C" Company to position of Right Support Company 1st East Lancashire Regiment.
    "B" Company to position of Left Support Company 1st East Lancashire Regiment. (already reconnoitred).
    "A" Company to position of Support Company of 9th Northumberland Fusiliers.
    "D" Company. To remain as at present disposed.

3. The necessary reconnaissances will be carried out forthwith.

4. ACKNOWLEDGE.

Capt and Adjt.
11th Bn. The Suffolk Regiment.

Copy 1 and 2. Retained.
    3 - 6. Companies.
    7. T.O.
    8. Q.M.
    9. Headquarters.
    10. 183rd Brigade (for information).

Appendix X

SECRET.   11th SUFFOLKS ORDER No. 66.   Copy No........

Ref: Sheet 36. N.W.   28.9.18.

1. The 11th Battalion Suffolk Regiment will withdraw to Divl Reserve in the MAURIANNE Area. tonight. The Battalion while in Divl Reserve will be the Line Battalion of the Southern Section of the Corps Battle Line as laid down in Defence Instructions attached.

2. Very Lights will be brought out. S.O.S. Grenades, Flares, paper Maps, etc and all documents connected with the Advanced Guard will be handed over by D Company and brought out by A, B and C Coys.

All Billet Stores, Trench Shelters, etc in new area will be taken over. Receipts for Stores handed over and taken over will be forwarded to Battalion H.Qrs by 9 a.m. on 29th inst.

3. Nucleus Garrisons in Corps Battle Line, (already reconnoitred) will be found by A Company. Remaining two platoons and Coy H.Q. will withdraw to billets in L.29.b. as arranged.

B and C Companies will withdraw after 8.30 p.m. to billets in L.29.b.

D Company will be relieved by B Coy 2/6th Bn. R. Warwicks, and on relief withdraw to billets in L.29.b.

4. Completion of relief or withdrawal will be notified to Bn.HQ. by the following code words :-
"A" Company.   12 seats.
"B"   "   6 seats.
"C"   "   3 seats.
"D"   "   Seats NIL.

Arrival in New Area will be reported by runner.

5. Quartermaster and Transport Officer will arrange to have Officers Valises, Mess Kit, Cookers, one per blanket per man in the new area, and a hot meal on arrival of troops.

Transport Officer will arrange for Company Comdrs Horses and one Limber per Company and Battn H.Qrs for transfer of Lewis Guns, Mess and Cooks Kit etc.

He will also arrange to deliver rations of the two forward platoons of A Coy as under :-
No.3. Platoon to Cross Roads NOUVEAU MONDE.
No.4. Platoon to ROUGE MAISON FARM.

6. All details, Drummers, Tailors, Shoemakers etc will rejoin the Battalion in the new area.

7. ACKNOWLEDGE.

                                    Captain & Adjutant.
                                    11th Bn SUFFOLK Regt.

Issued at 4 p.m.

Copy No. 1 and 2.   Retained.
         3 - 6   Coys.
         7 - 8   T.O. and Q.M.
         9 - 10   H.Qrs and R.S.M.
          11.   103rd Brigade.

SECRET.   DEFENCE INSTRUCTIONS.   Copy No......
                 NAU MONDE SECTION.

1. Nucleus garrisons, strength from 1 Section to 1 Platoon, will be provided by ~~the 1st E.Lancashire~~ Regt. to cover the following important points and main lines of approach :-
   (a) MUDDY LANE POST (G.33.c.1.5. and G.33.c.1.u.) This is a mixed platoon of 61st and 59th Divisions. ~~1st E.Lancs~~ A.Coy. will provide 2 Sections.
   The post will be under the command of an Officer detailed by ~~1st E.Lancashire Regt.~~ A.Coy.
   (b) NOUVEAU MONDE (G.27.c.3.2.) - 2 Roads.
   (c) G.27.c.4.5. - Road Bridge.
   (d) On high ground immediately EAST of Canal at G.21.d.7.0. This post will be responsible for footbridge at G.27.a.9.3 and road bridge at G.21.d.5.2. (PONT DE LA JUSTICE.
   (e) G.21.d.8.8.- 2 Road Bridges.- Post also to be responsible for footbridges at G.21.d.7.6. and G.21.b.95.60 respectively.
   Garrison will be a mixed platoon of right and left Brigades. 'A' Coy ~~1st E.Lancashire Regt.~~ will provide 2 Sections.
   Machine Guns are being placed in position to assist in covering the above points.
   The nucleus garrisons, with the exception of machine guns, may, when the tactical situation admits, be withdrawn during daytime for training. When not required for training, they should be allotted definite tasks for the maintenance and improvement of their posts.

2. The Battalion will on the order MAN BATTLE STATIONS be disposed as follows :-
   (a) B Company in the NOUVEAU MONDE locality.
       This Coy will man the following posts :-
           MUDDY LANE POST (G.33.c.1.5. & G.33.c.1.7.)
           NOUVEAU MONDE (G.27.c.7.8.)   XXXXXXXXXX
           G.27.c.4.5.
   (b) C Company in the HOLYHEAD (G.27.a) locality. This Company will be responsible for the houses on East side of the road from G.27.d.35.70 to G.27.b.2.6.
   (c) D Company in the old British defences about G.21 Central. This Company will man the posts at G.21.d.7.0. and G.21.d.8.8.
   (d) The nucleus garrisons found by "A" Company will on relief by B, C, and D Companies withdraw to area G.20.d. and be in Battalion Reserve.
   (e) Bn. H.Q. in G.20.d.

3. Acknowledge.

                                        C. Fanning
                                        Capt & Adjt
                                        11th Suffolk Regt

28.9.18.

Army Form C. 2118.

WAR DIARY
or
INTELLIGENCE SUMMARY.
(Erase heading not required.)

Vol 37

War Diary
11th (S.) Bn The Suffolk Regt (Cambs)
October 1st – 31st 1918.

WAR DIARY
or
INTELLIGENCE SUMMARY.
(Erase heading not required.)

Army Form C. 2118.

Place	Date	Hour	Summary of Events and Information	Remarks and references to Appendices
L.28.6.99 (Sect 36A)	Oct 1st		General Operation Instructions issued. Training continued.	Appendix I
	2		- Open Warfare exercises. Orders issued	Appendix I
BOESINGHEN	Oct 2		Proceeded to billets in BOESINGHEN by March Route.	Appendix II
	3		Training continued. Inspection of Stephinshish Rds. Gas Shin.	
	"4		Training continued (Open Warfare exercises)	Appendix III
	5		March to STERNBECQUE and Entrain for station at 0310 hours.	
HALLOY	6		Arrived in HALLOY at 1900 hours. B. Coy. at 0400 hours.	
	7		Training continued. In XVII Corps gen (B)H.Q. Reserve	
	8		First line transport by march to MOEUVRES - GRAINCOURT AREA.	
			Bn. orders - Exercises in action with Tanks.	
E.26.c.29	9		March to MOEUVRES & return to TERNIES. Bivouacked	Appendix IV
(Oct 5/6)			1000 yds E of MOEUVRES.	
H.E.	10		Bivouacked by CANTAING.	
I.B.& 7.2.	11		Training continued.	
	12		do.	
	13		do: (Church Parade & Ceremonies).	

WAR DIARY
or
INTELLIGENCE SUMMARY.
(Erase heading not required.)

Army Form C. 2118.

Instructions regarding War Diaries and Intelligence Summaries are contained in F. S. Regs., Part II. and the Staff Manual respectively. Title pages will be prepared in manuscript.

Place	Date	Hour	Summary of Events and Information	Remarks and references to Appendices
L.26.c.7.2.	14/10/00		Batt. Attack Scheme in Open Warfare in Co-operation with M.G.Bn. & L.T.M.B.	
	15 "		ditto	
	16 "		Salvaging.	
	17 "		Two coys. rested. Training continued. Salvage Remainder rested. Training continued.	
L.16.c.9.5.	18 "		March à brés — S. of CAMBRAI, & became Supporting	Appendix V.
(Ants) B.14)			Bgde. to Advanced Division	
	19 "		Training & Bn. Parade in morning. March to AVESNES-	
U.27.d.8.7.	20 "		LES — AUBERT. All in at 2300 hours.	Appendix VI.
(Shuts 51A S.W.)	21.		Inspection of Arms, Equipment, S.B.R., Battle Stores. Training — Outpost Schemes by day & night.	
	22.		Training continued.	
U.18.d. S.C.	23 "		March to ST. AUBERT, preparatory to Operations	Appendix VII.
		2038	Approach march to forming up position — in position by 0200	
MAISON BLEUE (Sheet 51A S.E.)	24.		Attack over river ECAILLON & secure high ground (King's 6. 179 and	Appendix VIII.

WAR DIARY
OR
INTELLIGENCE SUMMARY
(Erase heading not required.)

Army Form C. 2118.

Place	Date	Hour	Summary of Events and Information	Remarks and references to Appendices
	2/June/45		Ops ord. ZERO 0400. Objectives taken by 0545. Prisoners 2 Offrs, 98 O.R. 2 T.M's and abt 7 H.G's. Enemy heavily counter attacked. Leading Coy (B) who were forced to form defensive flank as Left Bde completely hung up unable to seize VENDOGIES. C Coy continued. Truck gained wk left about 1900 hours. Enemy withdrew from VENDOGIES during night under pressure from N. Line of objective established by 18th Bn. Early morning of 25 inst.	Appendix IX Appendix X
O.11.0.5.5.	25/6/44		Moved to ST. MARTIN and to follow to re-organise	
	26/6		Relieved 2/4 Ox & Bucks L.I. (184 Bde) in right sector (advanced Guard Brigade. Relief completed 0215.	Appendix XI
O.16.9.2.2	27/6			
O.6.C.2.4.	27/6	0500	Ordered to advance to ascertain enemy strength and form R. PRONFRUE, and of possible force passage and form Bridgehead. Silent June no shelling on both banks of river - Norkern Bank very strongly held	Appendix XI

WAR DIARY
or
INTELLIGENCE SUMMARY.

Army Form C. 2118.

Place	Date	Hour	Summary of Events and Information	Remarks and references to Appendices
		0700	by H.G's. A Coy. lost a Section over our left but all were killed before this could be exploited. Remainder driven back by H.G. fire, with many casualties. Occurred original position at 0730.	
		1300	Enemy very active — counter attack developed by our artillery. Heavy gas shelling of river valley at night. Relieved by 9th Bn Northumberland Fusiliers and in Kaba with Bn Support.	Appendix XII
Cita 4.2	28.10.18			
do.	29.10.18		Relieve 2/4 Ox. + Bucks L.I. in Corps Battle line. Direct hit on Bn HQ. (2 killed 8 wounded)	Appendix XIII
do.	30.10.18		Relieved by 2/6 Bn. R. War. Regt. & Corps Battle line re-occupied area vacated on 28th inst.	Appendix XIV
	31.10.18		Bridge & wire carrying parties for M.E.s in preparation of attack	
	1.11.18		"Stand To" at 05.15 for attack. C Coy. went forward	

WAR DIARY
or
INTELLIGENCE SUMMARY

Place	Date	Hour	Summary of Events and Information	Remarks and references to Appendices
To Support N.F's.				
			Casualties during month:	
			killed. wounded. wounded (no) Missing.	
			Officers 1 9 1	
			O.R's 37 194 19 13.	
15.11.18.				
			J.L. Firth Lt.Col.	
			Cmdg 11th(S) Bn. The Suffolk Regt.	

Secretary
War. Office (S.D.2)
London,

SECRET.   Copy No.......

Appendix I

11th Battn The SUFFOLK Regiment.
OPERATION INSTRUCTIONS PROVISIONAL.

Information (1) There are still indications of a possible further withdrawal of the enemy.

Intention. (2) On information being received as to the actual withdrawal of the enemy, as a result of reconnaisances in force or from other sources, the enemy will be immediately followed up by a vigorous renewal of our advance.

Objectives (3) The first objectives to be reached will be :-
ROAD JUNCTIONS H.33.d.40.10 - CROIX BLANCHE - FLEURBAIX. - ROUGE?? at point H.4.d.9.7. further objective will be the line LA BOUTELLERIE (exclusive) - BOIS GRENIER - RUE MARLE (exclusive).

Dispositions. (4) The Division will operate on a two Brigade front - 2 Battns in Line and one in Reserve.
Front Line Battalions disposed with :-
1 Company in Front Line.
2 Companies in Support.
1 Company in Reserve.

Accomodation in area evacuated by the enemy. (5) There is every reason to expect that the enemy has elaborated his system of mining dug-outs, buildings, cross roads etc, and it is therefore important that troops are warned beforehand to avoid all such places. H.Qrs of Battalions, Companies etc will not occupy dug-outs or buildings. Accomodation must be taken forward or improvised. The Q.M. will arrange to have three tents immediately available to go forward with Battn H.Qrs.   R.E. and Pioneers will be employed to examine and mark dug-outs etc.

Communication. (6) The Battn Intelligence Officer with observers will form an Advanced Report Centre to link up between Coys and H.Qrs.
Visual Signalling must be extensively used the Lucas Lamp especially. There is no restriction to the use of the lamp in a forward direction. Close touch maintained with flanks by means of liason units. Four Pigeons per Coy will be available.
Runners to be made use of as sparingly as possible.

Liason . (7) On receipt of orders Major G.West and mounted orderly will report to Bde H.Qrs for Liason Duty.

Supplies of S.A.A. (8) Sec-Lt C.W.R.Wilkins will act forthwith as assistant Transport Officer. His duty will be to keep close touch between Battn.H.Qrs and Transport to ensure efficient delivery of all supplies. All available Petrol Tins will be taken forward for water supply.

Equipment of Men. (9) When the Brigade next goes into the line the men will carry Packs and Overcoats. 170 rounds of S.A.A. and 2 Grenades per man will be carried, the latter to form a reserve for Rifle Grenadiers.

Very Lights S.O.S. etc. (10) Companies will ensure that they have an adequate supply of Very Lights, S.O.S. Grenades etc.
Very Lights Signals remain the same.
"A" For attack by the enemy - The S.O.S. Signal. present signal GREEN over GREEN over GREEN.
"B" To call for Supporting Fire. Red Very Lights.
"C" To lengthen Range.   do.
"D" To indicate position of our
       own Infantry.   White Very Lights.
"E" To shorten range.   Green Very Lights.

Transport. (11). On receipt of orders the T.O. will send :-
(a)   1 S.A.A. Limber complete with S.A.A. to Bde H.Qrs.   will be in charge of Bde Reserve of S.A.A.
(b)   2 Pack animals with Pack Saddles and the 4

SECRET.   Copy No........
            11th SUFFOLKS ORDERS No.   67.
Ref. Sheet 36 A.   2.10.18.

Appendix II

1. The Battn will march today to STEENBECQUE.
2. Starting Point. Battn.H.Qrs.
   Time.   0930 a.m.
   Order of March : Bn.H.Q. Drums, D,C,B,(A) Transport.
   Transport will all march together and will join the Battn at Q.M. Stores.
   A Coy will accompany the Battn if the 2 platoons in Corps Line have rejoined by then; otherwise it will follow as soon as possible with cooker and L.G.Limber.
   200 yds will be kept between Coys and between rear Coy and Transport and 25 yds between each six vehicles.
   Route : NEUF BERQUIN-MERVILLE and GOODWOOD HOUSE.
   Dress : Full Marching Order less Haversacks. Steel Helmets will be worn.
3. Besides the usual hourly halts there will be a halt at about 12.40 in J.11.b. for dinners.
4. A Billeting Party of 1 N.C.O. from Bn.H.Qrs and each Coy will report to Q.M. at Q.M.Stores at 0915 and will proceed on one of the lorries allotted to the Q.M., who will report to Staff Captain 183rd Bde at STEENBECQUE CHURCH at 1300.
5. Sick Parade. 7 a.m. (all men whom it is thought cannot
                        (march to attend.
   Breakfasts. 7.15 a.m.   report
6. The baggage wagons will be loaded at Q.M.Stores at 0900.
   Two lorries will report to the Q.M. at 0930.
   L.G.Limbers will be loaded by 0845.
   All Blankets and haversacks to be stacked by Guard by 0815.
   Mess Kit to be stacked by the Sergt Mess by 0845.
   Medical Stores to be stacked by the R.A.P. by 0845.
   All other baggage will be stacked by O.R. by 0815.
   The Q.M. and T.O. will arrange to collect the above.
7. ACKNOWLEDGE.

                                      Captain & Adjutant.
                                      11th SUFFOLK Regt.

   Issued at 4 a.m.

        1 - 2   Retained.
        3 - 6   Coys.
        7 - 8   T.O. and Q.M.
        9 - 10   H.Qrs and R.S.M.
          11   183rd Bde (For information).

2.

bandsmen now trained in the use of the YUKON
PACK to O.C. 103 L.T.M.B.

(c) Fighting portion of 1st Line Transport will
move with the Battalion i.e.
4 Lewis Gun Limbers.
6 S.A.A. and Grenade Limbers.
1 Limber (Pigs and Tools).
1 Maltese Cart.
6 Pack Animals.
(Pack saddles will be made up to 20 per Battn).
16 additional men will be allowed on Transport to
be trained on Pack Animal Work.

Prisoners of War Cage.
(12) On receipt of orders the Q.M. will send
1 N.C.O. and 3 O.R's from details etc to the
Prisoners of War cage at Farm L. 32.a.5.5. to
act as Guard.

Enemy T.M's.
(13) In the event of capture of hostile T.M's
the fact will be reported to Bn.H.Qrs without
delay, and a sentry placed over them to ensure
that they are not tampered with until taken over
by the Artillery.

Q.M. Stores.
(14) The Stores and Surplus Kit will remain in
present positions. If it becomes necessary to
remove Q.M.Stores a Surplus Kit dump will
be established at present Q.M. Stores 1st Battn
East Lancashire Regt.
The Q.M. will detail a man to be in charge of the
Battn surplus Kit in the event of the above move.
In the event of a forward move Trench Shelters
will be struck and if possible handed into D.A.D.O.S.
If time and Transport are not available they will
be dumped. Q.M. will leave a guard on such dump
and notify Staff Capt of locality and numbers so
dumped. He will also Staff Capt of the numbers
taken forward.

Captain & Adjutant.
11th SUFFOLK Regt.

SECRET.　　　　　　　　　　　　　　　　　　Appendix III
　　　　　　　　　　　　　　　　　　　　　　Copy No......1......
　　　　　　11th SUFFOLKS ORDER NO. 68.
　　　　　　-=-=-=-=-=-=-=-=-=-=-=-=-　　　5:10:18.

1. The Battalion will march to STEENBECQUE tomorrow morning and entrain there in accordance with table attached.
2. Dress : Full Marching Order. Steel Helmets will be worn. Waterbottles full.
3. Journey will take about 5 hours.
4. The Medical Officer will hold a special Sick Parade to which all men thought unfit to march are to be sent at 1800.
5. All baggage except Mess and Canteen will be stacked at Q.M. Stores by 18.30. The T.O. will arrange to collect blankets, Officers Kits, from the roadside if ready by 1800.
   Mess Kit and Canteen Stores will be fetched from Bn, Coy Messes and Canteen at 2100.
6. The Q.M. will arrange to send 3 guides to fetch Lorries from STEENBECQUE STATION at 23.55.
7. The Q.M. will arrange to have hot drinks served at STEENBECQUE STATION at 0310.
8. Entraining States will be rendered by Coy Comdrs, T.O. (to include all vehicles and animals) and O.i/c H.Qrs to O.R. by 1800. No damage and Clean billet certificates will be sent to O.R.
9. Lieut. S.J. Mason assisted by the Regtl Police will act as Bn Entraining Officer and will proceed with Transport to "mark off" train etc.
   2nd Lt P.E. Mothersole. M.M. has gone on to new area with billetting party.
10. ACKNOWLEDGE.

　　　　　　　　　　　　　　　　　　　　Captain & Adjutant,
　　　　　　　　　　　　　　　　　　　　11th SUFFOLKS.

　　　Copy No.1 and 2.　　Retained.
　　　　　　　3 - 6　　　　Coys.
　　　　　　　7 - 8　　　　T.O. and Q.M.
　　　　　　　9 - 10.　　　H.Qrs and R.S.M.
　　　　　　　11.　　　　　M.O.
　　　　　　　12.　　　　　185 Bde.

Appendix IV

SECRET.   Copy No............
                    11th SUFFOLKS ORDER NO.89.
                    ─────────────────────────   8.10.18.

Ref. Sheet 1/100,000, LENS 11.
              VALENCIENNES 12.

1. The Battalion will march to MONDICOURT tomorrow and entrain
   there in accordance with table attached.
2. Dress - Full Marching Order. Steel Helmets will be worn. Water
           Bottles Full.
3. Journey will take 4 to 5 hours.
3. Breakfasts - 06.00.
   Sick Parade - 06.30.
   The unexpired portion of the days rations (less Tea and Sugar)
   will be issued after breakfast and carried on the man.
X. The Camp Kettles used for breakfast will be at Q.M.Stores by
   09.00 and will be conveyed to train and used for tea on arrival at
   destination.
4. All Blankets and Officers rolls will be stacked at Q.M.Stores
   ready to load by 08.30.
   Mess Kit as arranged by Mess President.
5. The Q.M. will arrange for Guide for Lorry to be at Brigade H.Qrs.
   at 05.15 hours.
   Lorries will meet No.1 Train at destination.
6. All Billets will be ready for Inspection by 09.15.
7. Major G.West will act as Brigade Entraining Officer.
8. 2nd Lt F.E.Mothersole.H.M. assisted by Regtl Police will act
   as Battalion Entraining Officer and will mark off trains etc.
9. Lieut B.J.Mason, has gone to new area with billetting party.
   First Line Transport has proceeded to new area by March Route
   today.
10.   ACKNOWLEDGE.

                                      Captain & Adjutant.
                                      11th Bn The SUFFOLK Regt.

        Copy No.1 & 2.   Retained.
              3 - 6.   Companies.
                 7.   Battn.H.Qrs.
                 8.   Major G.West.
                 9.   Quartermaster.
                10.   Transport Officer.
                11.   R.S.M.
                12.   183rd Bde H.Qrs.

STARTING POINT.	TIME.	PASS BDE. STARTING POINT I.6.u.55.30	ARRIVE STATION.	TRAIN. NO.	TRAIN LEAVES.
TRANSPORT (less D. Coy Cooker). I.9.d.6.4.	24.01.	24.52.	01.10.	9.	04.10.
BATTALION (less Transport & D. Coy.) I.8.d.5.1. Order of march B.C.A. Coys. Sig. Mach.	02.05.	02.52.	03.10.	9.	04.10.
D COMPANY with Cooker & Team. I.9.d.6.4.	10.59.	11.52.	12.10.	10.	13.10.

SECRET.   11th SUFFOLKS Order No. 70.   Copy No.   Appendix V

Ref: 1/20,000 Sheet 57.C.N.E. and 57.B.N.W.   17.10.18.

1. The Battalion will march to billets SOUTH of CAMBRAI tomorrow 18th inst.
   Battn Parade L.4.a.6.1. at 0830 hours.
   Dress: Full Marching Order. Steel Helmets will be worn.
   On the march 100 yards distance will be maintained between Coys and Transport and 25 yards between each group of 6 vehicles.

2. One N.C.O. per Coy and Bn.H.Qrs and Transport will report to Major A.B.Wright.M.C. at 0745 hours. They will be provided with bicycles.

3. Baggage will be stacked ready for loading at 0730 as under:-
   Blankets, tightly rolled in tens at L.4.a.9.4.
   Valises at L.4.a.6.0.
   Mess Kit at Bn.H.Qrs.
   L.G. Limbers will be loaded at L.4.a.6.0.

4. Trench Shelters will be handed over.
   The Regtl Police will act as guards to the Camp and Lieut.H. Williamson will hand over and obtain recipts and clean billet certificates.

5. Transport will move complete to establishment.

6. The Q.M. will arrange for a guide to meet lorry for blankets at Bde H.Qrs 0820.

7. ACKNOWLEDGE.

Capt & Adjutant.
11th SUFFOLKS.

Copy No.1 and 2.   Retained.   3 - 6   Coys.
        7 - 8   T.O. and Q.M.   9 - 10   H.Qrs and Sig Off.
        11 - 12   R.S.M. and M.O. 1w/   183rd Bde.

SECRET

Appendix - VI.

Copy No. 1.

11th SUFFOLKS ORDER No. 71
19-10-18.

Ref Sheet 1/2000 57. B. N.W.
1/2000 51. A. S.W.

1. The Bn. less Transport will march to AVESNES-LEZ-AUBERT tonight.
Parade in column of route, head of column at A. Coys' H.Q. at 18.50 hours.
Order of march H.Q., A, B, C, & D. Coys.
Dress - Full Marching Order. Steel Helmets will be worn.
On the march 50 yds distance will be maintained between Coys.

2. The Transport will follow on Bde. Transport. Starting Point - Cross Rds A.17.C. Central. Time 20.04. On the march 100 yds distance will be maintained between Battn. Transports.
The following will proceed with Transport.
1 Lewis Gunner per Coy.
2 Cooks per Coy.
1 N.C.O. & 3 men of H.Q. AA Section.

3. Baggage, Lewis Guns, Cooks Kit, etc., will be loaded at Transport by 18.30.

4. Billeting Party & Guides have already proceeded.

5. Clean Billet Certificates will be obtained from incoming Battalion & sent to Orderly Room by 0900 hours 20th inst.

6. ACKNOWLEDGE.

Capt. & Adjt.
11th SUFFOLK REGT.

Copy No. 1 & 2. Retained
3 - 6. Companies
7. H.Qs.
8. Q.M.
9. T.O.
10. RSM

Appendix VII

SECRET.   Copy No.

11th SUFFOLKS ORDER NO 72.

Ref.Map 1/40,000.Sheet.51 A.   22.10.18.

1. The Battalion will march to ST AUBERT tomorrow, the 23rd inst as under, preparatory to operations on the 24th inst.

   Starting Point U.28.a.03.
   Time 0935. Order of march: Hdqrs, "A", "B", "C", "D", Transport.

2. Billetting Party under Major A.B.Wright, M.C., has gone forward.

3. Blankets etc will be stacked at Q.M. Stores at 0730.

4. ACKNOWLEDGE.

                                                    Capt and Adjutant.

   Copy 1 and 2. Retained.
         3 - 6. Companies.
         7.   Bn.Hdqrs.
         8.   Q.M.
         9.   T.O.
        10.   R.S.M.

SECRET.   Copy No.......
                    Appendix VII.
              11th SUFFOLKS ORDER NO. 73.
              -=-=-=-=-=-=-=-=-=-=-=-=-=-   23.10.18.
Ref. Sheet 51A. S.E.1/20,000.
1.   The Battalion will pass through the present outpost line
     (BROWN LINE) and attack and capture the high ground running
     through Q.17.a. and 10.b.& d. Central.
     Battalion Right Boundary - Cross Roads Q.31.a.0.0 - Mill Q.26.d.
     2.4 - W. edge of ST MARTIN (Q.21.c.7.1½) - Cross Roads Q.22.a.3.8.
     - Junction of Stream and road Q.17.a.1.9. (Note - Copse in
     Q.16.b. inclusive to Battalion) Compass bearing for General Line
     of the advance is 58° M.
     Battalion Left Boundary - Cross Roads Q.25.c.0.1. - N.E. along
     road to Road Junction Q.19.d.7.7. - la PLANCHE a PIERRE (inclusi-
     Road and River Junction Q.20.a.9.8 (inclusive) - Cross Roads Q.14.
     d.8.1. (inclusive) - Road and River Junction Q.19.a.0.7.
     Inter Company Boundary will be a line through Cross Roads Q.16.
     a.3.2 running parallel to Battalion Boundaries. The Cross Roads
     to be inclusive to B.Coy.
     A Main Line of Resistance will be established on the reverse
     slope of the Ridge running through Q.16.c. - Q.23.a by the C.
     (Southern), D. (Northern) Companies.
     The Outpost Line of Resistance will be established on the
     reverse slope of the ridge running through Q.17.a. - Q.10.b.& d.
     by A. & B. Companies.
2.   A. Company will be Right Front Company.
     B.   ..   ..   .. Left   ..   ..
     C.   ..   ..   .. Support ..
     D.   ..   ..   .. Reserve ..
3.   Battalion H.Qs. will be established at MAISON BLEUE with an
     Advanced Report Centre on W. Edge of ST MARTIN as the attack
     developes. H.Qs. will then bound to the Advanced Report Centre
     which will move to Q.16.c.00.25, and, if necessary, to E. edge
     of Copse in Q.16.b.
     The Signal Officer will establish telephone communication from
     Battalion and Report Centre to Brigade Report Centre at P.36.b.8.
     3., and Visual with all Companies.
     A White Very Light fired in the direction of the enemy will
     indicate "we are here".
     A Contact Aeroplane will be over at 07.30, 09.00 and 11.00
     hours. On the call for flares the foremost troops will immediate-
     ly light flares to indicate their position.
4.   ARTILLERY. - As per Barrage Table issued ti Coy. Comdrs.
5.   MACHINE GUNS. One Section, C.Company, 61st M.G.Bn. is allotted
     to the Battalion.
6.   L.T.M. - 2 Guns of 183rd L.T.M.B. are allotted to the Battn.
     and will be attached to C.Company.
7.   R.E. & PIONEERS. - Pioneer Parties will carry light Foot
     Bridges, which will be allotted as under :-
          1 Bridge to be in position at the MILL.
          1 Bridge to be in position at the FM d'ORCHIVAL.
          1 Bridge each to A. & B. Companies for crossing ECAILLON RIVER.
8.   AID POST. R.A.P. will be established at Battalion H.Qs.,
     and will bound forward at same time.
          A.D.S. - HAUSSY (V.14.d.9.2.)
                   MONTRECOURT (P.34.c.3.2.)
     Eight R.A.M.C. Bearers with two Runners will report to M.O.
9.   The Transport Officer will arrange for following L.G.Limbers
     to accompany each Company as far as possible. 1 Limber and 4
     Pack Animals to accompany Battalion H.Qs., the limber will contain
     a reserve of S.A.A., V.P.A., S.O.S., Flares, etc.
     1 Limber complete with S.A.A. to report to the Staff Captain
     at ST AUBERT. This Limber will form part of Brigade Reserve.
10. Nucleus and Surplus Personnel will report to Major A.B.Wright,
     M.C. at the Q.M.Stores at 19.30 hours.

- 2 -

11. The Q.M. will arrange for a hot drink to be served to Coys. on the march up to assembly positions.
12. ZERO Hour will be 04.00 hours, 24th inst.
13. ACKNOWLEDGE.

Captain and Adjutant,
Issued at 19.45.   11th Battalion THE SUFFOLK REGT.

Copy No. 1 & 2 Retained.
        3 - 6 Companies.
        7 Intelligence Officer.
        8 Signalling Officer.
        9 Quartermaster.
       10 Transport Officer.
       11 A/R.S.M.
       12 183 Brigade.

SECRET.   Appendix IX
                                                              Copy No.......
                    11th SUFFOLKS ORDER NO. 74.
                  -=-=-=-=-=-=-=-=-=-=-=-=-=-=-   25.10.18.
Ref.Sheet 51.A. S.E.
1.   The Battalion will move forward as Support Brigade forthwith,
     and take up position as Brigade Reserve in LA FOLIE Area.
2.   D.Company will be Right Front Company.
        C.   ..   .. .. Left   ..   ..
        B.   ..   .. .. Right Support   ..
        A.   ,, ... Left   ..   ..
        Battalion H.Qs. will be at Q.22.a.5.3.
3.   Completion of assembly will be reported to Battn.H.Qs. by
     Runner.
4.   ACKNOWLEDGE.

                                                    [signature]

                                             Captain and Adjutant,
Issued at 10.00.   11th Battalion THE SUFFOLK REGT.

        Copy No. 1 & 2 Retained.
                 3 - 6 Companies.
                 7   Intelligence Officer.
                 8   Signalling Officer.
                 9   Quartermaster.
                10   Transport Officer.
                11   A/R.S.M.
                12   183 Brigade.

Appendix X

SECRET.　　　　　　　　　　　　　　　　　　　　　　　Copy No..........

11th SUFFOLKS ORDER NO. 75.　　　　　26.10.18.

Ref. Sheet 51A. S.E.
　"　　"　51A. N.E.

1. The Battalion will relieve the 2/4th Oxford & Bucks L.I. as Right Battalion of the Advanced Guard Brigade tonight.
2. B. Company will be Right Company.
　　D.　"　　"　"　Centre　"
　　C.　"　　"　"　Left　"
　　A.　"　　"　"　Support　"
　　Battalion H.Qs. will be at LARBLIN Q.16.a.4.2. with advanced H.Qs. at Q.9.b.2.4.
3. Relief complete will be reported by the code word "SWOP".
4. ACKNOWLEDGE.

　　　　　　　　　　　　　　　　　　　　　Captain and Adjutant,
Issued at 18.00.　　　　　　　　　11th Battalion THE SUFFOLK REGT.

Copy No. 1 & 2 Retained.
　　　　　3 - 6　Companies.
　　　　　7　　Intelligence Officer.
　　　　　8　　Signalling Officer.
　　　　　9　　Quartermaster.
　　　　10　　Transport Officer.
　　　　11　　A/R.S.M.
　　　　12　　183 Brigade.

SECRET.

Appendix XII
Copy No..........

11th SUFFOLKS ORDER NO. 77.

28.10.18.

Ref. Sketch Map (VENDEGIES)

1. The Battalion will be relieved tonight by the 9th Northd. Fus. and on relief will withdraw to area Q.10.b & d, Q.11.c.
2. Companies will bring out Pouch Ammn. (complete), Very Lights, Flares, S.O.S.Grenades, Bombs and Tools. Box and Surplus Ammn. will be handed over.
3. Five Guides per Company will assemble at Advanced Battalion H.Qs. at 16.30 and will be taken by the I.O. to meet incoming Battalion at Q.6.d.central at 17.00 hours.
4. Guides will meet Companies after relief at Road Junction Q.11.d.0.2. to take them to new area.
5. Battalion H.Qs. will be at LARBLIN.
6. Companies will report -
   1. When relieved by code word "FIN".
   2. On arrival in new area by Runner.
7. ACKNOWLEDGE.

Issued at 16.00 hours.

Captain and Adjutant,
11th Battalion THE SUFFOLK REGT.

Copy No.1 & 2 Retained.
    3 - 6 Companies.
    7. Intelligence Officer.
    8. Signalling Officer.
    9. Quartermaster.
    10. Transport Officer.
    11. A/R.S.M.
    12. 183 Brigade.

Appendix XIII

SECRET.   Copy No.....1......

        11th SUFFOLKS ORDER No. 78.
--------------------------------   29.10.18.

1. The Battalion will relieve the 2/4th Oxford & Bucks L.I. in the Corps Battle Line.
   D. Company will be Right Front Company near LA JUSTICE
   C.   "   "   " Left   "   "   LES COPSE
   B.   "   "   " Right Support   "   4.3.a.
   A.   "   "   " Left   "   4.3.d.
   Battalion H.Qs. will remain in present location.
2. Guides at the rate of 5 per Coy. will be at the CHAPEL 4.10.c.7.9 to pick up Companies as follows :-
   C. Company   ..   16.45.
   A.   "   ..   16.50.
   D.   "   ..   16.55.
   B.   "   ..   17.00.
   Companies will move by Platoons at 100^x distance.
3. Completion of relief will be reported by Runner.
4. ACKNOWLEDGE.

                                            Captain and Adjutant,
Issued at 16.00.   11th Battalion THE SUFFOLK REGT.

Copy No. 1 & 2 Retained.
       3 - 6 Companies.
       7. Intelligence Officer.
       8. Signalling Officer.
       9. Quartermaster.
      10. Transport Officer.
      11. A/R.S.M.
      12. 183 Brigade.

SECRET.   Appendix XIV
                                                                    Copy No.............

                        11th SUFFOLKS ORDER No. 79.
                        -=-=-=-=-=-=-=-=-=-=-=-=-=-   30.10.18.

1.   The 2/6th Royal Warwickshire Regt. will relieve the Battalion
   in present area as under :-
        B.Company R.War. relieves C.Company 11th Suffolks.
        A.   ..   ..   ..   D.   ..   ..
        D.   ..   ..   ..   A & B Coys.   ..
        A & B Companies will be relieved about 15.30 hours. C & D
   Companies about 18.00 hours.
2.   On relief Companies will re-occupy areas vacated yesterday.
3.   Guides will only be required from C.Company (1 per Platoon)
   who will meet incoming troops at Road Junction-Q.8.b.7.2 at
   17.30 hours.
4.   Relief complete to be reported by Runner to present H.Qs.
5.   ACKNOWLEDGE.

                                                Captain and Adjutant,
Issued at 14.00.   11th Battalion THE SUFFOLK REGT.

Copy No. 1 & 2 Retained.
         3 - 6 Companies.
         7. Intelligence Officer.
         8. Signalling Officer.
         9. Quartermaster.
        10. Transport Officer.
        11. A/R.S.M.
        12. 183 Brigade.

SECRET.

Appendix XI
Copy No............

11th SUFFOLKS ORDER NO. 76.

27.10.18.

Ref. Sheet 51A.S.E.
51A.N.E.

1. The Battalion will advance and endeavour to force a passage over the R.RHONELLE and form a Bridge head about L.26.c & d., N.E. of MARESCHES.

2. D.Company will endeavour to cross about L.32.b.1.9.
   C.Company will endeavour to cross about L.25.d.o.4.
   B. & A.Companies will be in Support.
   Battalion H.Qs. will be at Q.6.b.2.4.

3. If the Bridgehead is secured, artillery barrage will open at 08.30 hours under cover of which the advance will be continued to secure the high ground about L.27.a & b and L.21.c.

4. ACKNOWLEDGE.

Waining
Captain and Adjutant,
11th Battalion THE SUFFOLK REGT.

Issued at 02.30.

Copy No. 1 & 2 Retained.
    3 - 6 Companies.
    7. Intelligence Officer.
    8. Signalling   ..
    9. Quartermaster.
   10. Transport Officer.
   11. A/R.S.M.
   12. 183 Brigade.

Field Survey Bn. [10884]. 23-10-18:   Scale 1 : 40,000.   YARDS 1000 0 1000 2000 YARDS   Part of 51a.

REFERENCE SKETCH ON BACK

To _____

1. MY {PLATOON / COMPANY} HAS REACHED _____ (MARK POSITION ON MAP OR GIVE MAP REFERENCE)

   AND IS CONSOLIDATING _____
   HAS CONSOLIDATED _____
   IS READY TO ADVANCE _____

2. I AM (NOT) IN TOUCH WITH _____ ON RIGHT
   AND (NOT) WITH _____ ON LEFT

3. I AM HELD UP AT _____ BY WIRE
   BY M.G. FIRE
   BY RIFLE FIRE.

4. ENEMY'S ARTILLERY IS FIRING ON _____
   FROM _____

5. I HAVE SENT FORWARD PATROLS TO _____

6. I ESTIMATE { MY CASUALTIES AT _____
   MY STRENGTH AT _____

7. I NEED
   BOXES S.A.A.
   LEWIS GUN DRUMS
   BOMBS
   RIFLE GRENADES
   STOKES SHELLS   (AT ONCE)
   VERY LIGHTS
   GROUND FLARES   (TO NIGHT)
   STAKES
   COILS WIRE
   TINS WATER
   RATIONS

8. I INTEND TO _____

9. (GENERAL REMARKS ON POSITION AND STRENGTH OF ENEMY. NUMBER OF PRISONERS TAKEN AND IDENTIFICATIONS IF KNOWN).

TIME _____ NAME _____ RANK _____
DATE _____ PLATOON _____ COY. _____
BATTALION _____

STRIKE OUT ALL THAT IS NOT APPLICABLE AND FORWARD AT ONCE TO BN. H.Q.

WAR DIARY
or
INTELLIGENCE SUMMARY.

Army Form C. 2118.

War Diary
11th (S) Bn the Suffolk Regt
(Cambs)
November 1st – 30th 1918.

WAR DIARY
or
INTELLIGENCE SUMMARY.
(Erase heading not required.)

Army Form C. 2118.

Place	Date	Hour	Summary of Events and Information	Remarks and references to Appendices
Q.16.a.4.2. (Vendhuile)	1/11/18	0515	Stand To" ready to support attack on high ground in L.27 a.& c. & L.21.c. Attack successful. C. Coy sent forward in support of Tank M.E's	Appendix I
SONCHING	2/11/18	1500	Bn. ordered to billets in SONCHING in Reserve.	
AESNES	2/11/18	0825	Proceed by March Route to AESNES - 6.45 AUBERT. Arrived Appendix II	Appendix II
-les-AUBERT			in billets 13.45.	
	3.11.18		Men rested & bathed. Draft of 167 O.R's received. Cleaning up & re-organisation. Concert in afternoon by	
	4.11.18		Divl. Concert Party.	
	5.11.18		Training - games. S.B.R Inspection by Bde Gas Officer.	
	6.11.18		Training continued. Lewis Guns & Rifles are revised by Staff Armourer	
	7.11.18		Training continued.	
BERNERAIN	8.11.18		March to BERNERAIN. All in billets 1600 hours.	Appendix III
	9.11.18		Training continued	
	10.11.18		Church Parade. Night operations - Advance to Attack Scheme.	

WAR DIARY
or
INTELLIGENCE SUMMARY.
(Erase heading not required.)

Army Form C. 2118.

Place	Date	Hour	Summary of Events and Information	Remarks and references to Appendices
BERNAPAIN	11/11/18		Training continued. Bn. attack scheme. Telegram from Adv. XVII Corps "Hostilities will cease 1100 hours today 20. Where Troops will stand fast on line reached at that hour, which will be reported by wire to Corps H.Q.rs. Defensive precaution will be maintained and there will be no intercourse of any description with the enemy area."	
	12/11/18		Training continued – general sweeping up.	
	13/11/18		do. Ceremonial of R. Scots. Arms drill &c.	
ST. HUBERT	14/11/18		March to ST HUBERT. Starting point 10.2. All in billets	Appendix IV
		13.20	Special Order of the Day issued – message from the Lieutenant of Cambridgeshire	Appendix V
CAMBRAI	16/11/18		March to CAMBRAI. Starting point 10.50. All in billets 1600 hours.	Appendix VI
	17/11/18		Cleaning of billets. Ceremonial drill by Coys. Bde. Church Parade – JARDIN DE L'ESPLANADE	

WAR DIARY or INTELLIGENCE SUMMARY

Army Form C. 2118.

Place	Date	Hour	Summary of Events and Information	Remarks and references to Appendices
CAMBRAI	17.11.18		Baths.	
	18.11.18		Training continued. Ceremonial Bn. Drill parade.	
	19.11.18		do. Inspection of billets by B.G.C. parent.	
	20.11.18		do.	
	21.11.18		do. Route March. Lecture on "Demobilisation".	
	22.11.18		Salvage work – Fumay area.	
	23.11.18		Salvage work. Transport less party proceeding to BERNAVILLE area by march route.	Appendix VII.
			Ptrain proceed to BERNAVILLE area by march route.	
	24.11.18		Church Parade. Lecture to Voters.	
	~~25.11.18~~		Entrain at CAMBRAI VILLE to CONTEVILLE 23.30 hours	Appendix VIII.
	25.11.18		Arrived at Station Siding at 16.00 hours eventually (per order by Entraining officer) & left at 20.50 hours. Arrived at CONTEVILLE at 15.45. 26 First (Journey fined by Sigh) hours approx) marched to billets – A.T.C. Coy to MONTIGNY. D. Coy to GRIMONT, B.Coy. H.Q's & transport to HEUZECOURT. All in billets by 20.30 hours.	
HEUZECOURT 26.11.18 (LENS II)				

WAR DIARY
or
INTELLIGENCE SUMMARY.
(Erase heading not required.)

Army Form C. 2118.

Place	Date	Hour	Summary of Events and Information	Remarks and references to Appendices
HEUDECOURT	27/11/18		Incoming billets, which are very bad.	
	28/11/18		do. Cleaning up	
	29/11/18		do. Rest – training in billets	
	30/11/18		Route March.	
			Honours during Month.	
			328457 Sgt. DE JEFFERY Croix de Guerre	
			20535 Sgt. J. CHAPLA Military Medal	
			325190 Sgt. F. HAMAS do.	
			3/10325 Sgt. A. READER do.	
			16668 Cpl. G.H. WILLING do.	
			42605 Cpl. A.E. SPURGEON do.	
			40253 Cpl. R.A. JENNINGS do.	
			141194 Cpl. W.H. GILLINGHAM do.	
			4220 L/Cpl. G.M. FAIRCLOUGH do.	
			24072 Pte. P. WOODS do.	
			9296 Pte. R. CORBIN do.	
			42158 Pte. G. HEATH do.	
			15360 Pte. G. TITCHMARSH do.	
			42146 Pte. W. BROOM do.	
			41234 Pte. W.H. KELLY do.	
			12533 C.S.M. C. CAUSTON D.C.M.	
			8914 C.Q.M.S. W.E. MANN M.M. D.C.M.	
			Casualties during month.	
			OFF. O.R's.
			Killed	
			Wounded	
			Wounded (gas)	
			Missing, believed killed	
			M/Capt. H.J.P. CREAGH. Military Cross.	
			Revd. W.C. GENTLE do.	
			Revd. G. TURNER. do.	
			Capt. G.F.R. Sandy M.C. Bar to Military Cross	
			Capt. S.W. TURNER R.M.C. do.	
			L.N. Turner Lt. Col	
			Comdg. 11th Bn. The Suffolk Regt.	

Appendix II

SECRET.　　　　　　　　　　　　　　　　　　　　　　　Copy No..........

11th SUFFOLKS ORDER NO. 81.　　　　　　4.11.18.

Ref.Sheet 51.A. S.W.
1. The Battalion will march to AVESNES-les-AUBERT.
2. Parade in Column of Route - head of column at Road Junction Q.7.d.Central at 08.25 hours.
   Order of March - C.Company, H.Qs., A., B., and D.Companies.
3. The Transport, Details and Band will join column at Cross Roads P.24.c.9.1. at 09.00 hours.
4. Arrival in Billets will be reported by Runner.
5. ACKNOWLEDGE.

　　　　　　　　　　　　　　　　　　　　　Captain and Adjutant,
Issued at 22.00.　　　　　　　　　　　11th Battalion THE SUFFOLK REGT.

Copy No. 1 & 2 Retained.
　　　　　3 - 6 Companies.
　　　　　7. Intelligence Officer.
　　　　　8. Signalling Officer.
　　　　　9. Quartermaster.
　　　　10. Transport Officer.
　　　　11. A/R.S.M.
　　　　12. 183 Brigade.

SECRET.   Copy No. Appendix III

11th SUFFOLKS ORDER NO. 82.

                                                                8.11.18.

Ref. Sheet 51.A.

1. The Battalion will march tomorrow to BERMERAIN Area.

2. Parade in Column of Route with Head of Column at A.Coy.H.Qs.
    in order H.Qs., A., B., C., D. at 11.30 hours.
    Dress - Full Marching Order, Steel Helmets will be worn.

3. On the march usual distances and halts will be observed.

4. Breakfasts - 06.45 hours.
    Sick Parade - 07.30 (Full Marching Order).

5. Blankets tightly rolled in tens and all baggage to be at
    Q.M.Stores by 07.30 hours.

6. 1 N.C.O. per Coy. and Battn. H.Qs. will report at the
    Orderly Room at 07.30 hours and proceed on bicycles under
    Major A.B.Wright, M.C. as a billetting party to meet the
    Staff Captain 183rd Brigade at BERMERAIN CHURCH at 09.30.

7. Billets will be ready for inspection by 11.00 hours.

8. ACKNOWLEDGE.

                                                    [signature]

                                                Captain and Adjutant,
Issued at 23.00.   11th Battalion THE SUFFOLK REGT.

Copy No. 1 & 2 Retained.
        3 - 6 Companies.
        7. Battalion H.Qs.
        8. Quartermaster.
        9. Transport Officer.
       10. Major A.B.Wright, M.C.
       11. Major G.West.
       12. 183rd Brigade.

SECRET.

Appendix IV.

Copy No. ....

11th SUFFOLKS ORDER No. 83.

13:11:18.

Ref. Sheet 51.A.

1. The Battalion will march tomorrow to ~~AVESNES LES~~ ST AUBERT.
2. Parade in Column of Route with Head of Column at Bn.H.Qs. Billet in order H.Qs., Drummers, C., D., A., B. at 10.00 hours. Dress - Full Marching Order, Steel Helmets will be worn.
3. On the march usual distances and halts will be observed.
4. Breakfasts - 07.45 hours.
   Sick Parade - 09.00 hours. (Full Marching Order).
5. Blankets tightly rolled in tens and all baggage to be at the Q.M.Stores by 09.00 hours.
6. 1 N.C.O. per Coy. and Battn. H.Qs. will report at the Orderly Room at 07.30 hours and proceed on bicycles under Major A.B.Wright, M.C. as a billeting party to meet the Staff Captain 183rd Brigade at the Town Majors' Office, ST AUBERT at 09.00 hours.
7. Billets will be ready for inspection by 09.30 hours.
8. ACKNOWLEDGE.

Captain and Adjutant,
Issued at 23.30 hours.   11th Battalion THE SUFFOLK REGT.

Copy No. 1 & 2 Retained.
    3 - 6 Companies.
    7. Battalion H.Qs.
    8. Quartermaster.
    9. Transport Officer.
    10. Major A.B.Wright, M.C.
    11. R.S.M.
    12. 183rd Brigade.

SECRET.   Copy No..........

              11th SUFFOLKS ORDER No. 80.
              -=-=-=-=-=-=-=-=-=-=   1.11.18.

Ref. Sheet 51.A.
1.   The Battalion less C.Company will withdraw at dusk, and
     proceed to Billets in SOMAING.
2.   Guides will meet Companies at SOMAING CHURCH and guide
     them to Billets.
3.   Companies will move at the following times :-
              A.Company   17.30 hours.
              B.   "   17.40   "
              D.   "   17.50   "
4.   C.Company after relief will pass from the command of 9th Bn.
     Northd. Fus. and rejoin Battalion at SOMAING.
5.   ACKNOWLEDGE.

                                      Captain and Adjutant,
Issued at 15.00.   11th Battalion THE SUFFOLK REGT.

Copy No. 1 & 2 Retained
         3 - 6 Companies.
         7. Intelligence Officer.
         8. Signalling Officer.
         9. Quartermaster.
        10. Transport Officer.
        11. A/R.S.M.
        12. 183 Brigade.

Appendix V.

SPECIAL ORDER OF THE DAY.

By LIEUT. COLONEL. G.L.J. TUCK., D.S.O.,

Commanding 11th Battalion. THE SUFFOLK REGT.

The following message and reply is published for the information of all ranks:-

TO :- O.C.,
    11th Battalion THE SUFFOLK REGT. (Cambridgeshire)
    B.E.F., France.

On behalf of the County and Isle Hearty Congratulations on the Glorious Victory to which you have contributed so much.

(Signed). ADEANE,
LORD LIEUT. OF CAMBRIDGESHIRE.

Nov. 11th, 1918.

To:- LORD LIEUT OF CAMBRIDGESHIRE.

CAMBRIDGESHIRE BATTALION SUFFOLK REGIMENT much appreciate your message and Battalion is proud to have represented COUNTY and ISLE in last smashing blow.

(Signed). TUCK.,
Commanding CAMBRIDGESHIRE BATTALION
SUFFOLK REGIMENT.

Field.
Nov. 11th, 1918.

Captain and Adjt.
11th Bn. THE SUFFOLK REGIMENT.

14.11.18.,

SECRET.

Appendix VI.

Copy No.

11th SUFFOLKS ORDER NO 84.

15.11.18.

Reference:- Sheet 51.A.
" 57.B.

1. The Battalion will march today to CAMBRAI.(N.E.Area).

2. Parade in column of route with head of column at Cross-Roads U.18.d.6.0. in order:- Hdqrs,Drums,"D","C","B","A", at 1050 hours.
Dress :- Full Marching Order. Caps.S.D.will be worn. Steel Helmets carried on the back of the pack.

3. On the march usual distances and halts will be observed.

4. Breakfast 0745 hours. Sick Parade 0800 hours.(Full Marching Order).

5. Blankets tightly rolled in tens and all baggage to be at the Q.M. Stores by 0930 hours. Transport Officer will arrange to collect Officers Valises from all billets, also Officers Mess Kit.

6. 1 N.C.O per Company and Battalion Headquarters will report to the Orderly Room at 0745 hours and proceed on bicycles and proceed under Major A.B.Wright,M.C., as a Billeting Party to meet the Staff Captain 183 Brigade at the Town Commandants Office CAMBRAI TOWN at 0915 hours.

7. Billets will be ready for inspection by 1015 hours.

8. ACKNOWLEDGE.

Issued at 0100 hours.

Capt and Adjutant.
11th Bn.THE SUFFOLK REGT.

Copy No 1 and 2 - Retained.
    3 - 6. - Companies.
      7. - Bn.Hdqrs.
      8. - Q.M.
      9. - T.O.
     10. - Major A.B.Wright.M.C.,
     11. - M.O.
     12. - R.S.M.
     13. - 183 Brigade.

Appendix VII

11th SUFFOLKS ORDER NO. 85.

Ref. 57B.N.W. 1/20000
VALENCIENNES 1/100,000.

To T.O.   22.11.18.
    Q.M.
    & G.O.

The Bn. Transport, less 4 Cookers, 1 Water Cart, Mess Cart, 1 Baggage wagon, Officers Chargers & necessary Personnel, will proceed by March Route tomorrow to BERNAVILLE area.

Starting Point – Rd. junction A.11.d.8.3.

Time 0803.

Route. Bridge at A.11.c.4.2. – Water Tower – JARDIN le d'ESPLANADE – MASNIÈRES RD.

Transport will move complete to Establishment.

Water Cart will travel full.

                            [signature]
                            Capt.
22.11.18.   11th Bn. The Suffolk Rgt.

SECRET.   Copy No...........
    11th SUFFOLKS ORDER No. 86.
    ---------------------------   23.11.18.

Ref.Sheets 57.B. N.W. 1/20,000   Appendix VIII.
    VALENCIENNES 1/100,000.
    LENS   ...   1/100,000.

1. The Battalion, less Transport travelling by Road, will entrain at CAMBRAI VILLE on 24th/25th inst. as shown on Table attached. The journey will take approximately 8 hours.

2. The Battalion, less Transport travelling by Rail, will parade in Column of Route on S. side of RUE LE CATEAU in order H.Qs., Drums, A., B., C., D. Coys. Head of Column at A.Coys' H.Qs.
Time - 05.10 - 25th inst.
Dress.- Full Marching Order, plus 1 Blanket rolled on top of pack.

3. Transport proceeding by Rail will parade on N. side of RUE LE CATEAU by stables at 21.10 - 24th inst.
O.C. Coys. will detail 1 Cook to proceed with Coy. Cooker, and 1 Officers' Mess Servant to proceed with Mess Cart.

4. The Quartermaster will arrange for Guide to meet Lorry and for Guard for Stores etc.
He will also arrange for Hot Tea to be served at Entraining Station and for Cookers to prepare a meal on arrival at Detraining Station.

5. Blankets (less 1 per man) and all Stores will be stacked at the Q.M.Stores, tightly rolled in bundles of tens, ready to load by 18.30 hours 24th inst.

6. Officers' Valises will be ready for collection by 18.30 hours.

- 2 -

7. Lieut.H.Williamson will act as Battalion Entraining Officer.
8. Capt.G.J.Pytchen will act as Detraining Officer for the 3 Trains of the Brigade Group. He will travel on No.4 Train.
9. ACKNOWLEDGE.

[signature]

Captain and Adjutant,
11th Battalion THE SUFFOLK REGT.

Issued at 20.00 hours.

Copy No. 1 & 2 Retained.
   3 - 6 Companies.
   7. Battalion H.Q.
   8. Quartermaster.
   9. Transport Officer.
   10. Capt.G.J.Pytchen.
   11. Medical Officer.
   12. R.S.M.
   13. 103rd Brigade.

Copy No.

AMENDMENT to 11th SUFFOLK ORDER NO 86.

1. <u>PARA. 2.</u>

    Battalion, less Transport travelling by rail, will now parade as ordered at <u>23.10.</u> and will travel on Train No 4.

2. <u>PARA 3.</u>

    Transport proceeding by rail will now parade as ordered at <u>00.10.</u> 25th inst, and will travel on Train No 5.

    <u>ACKNOWLEDGE.</u>

    Capt and Adjutant.

24.11.18.   11th (S).Bn.The Suffolk Regiment.(Cambs).

No. of Train.	Date.	Entraining Station.	Time.	Train departs.	Detraining Station.	Time of arrival.
4.	24th.	CAMBRAI VILLE.	21.30.	00.55.	CONTEVILLE.	08.00.
3.	25th.	do.	03.30.	04.55.	do.	12.00.

WAR DIARY.

11th (S) Bn. The Suffolk Regt.

December 1st – 31st 1918.

Army Form C. 2118.

WO 39

Army Form C. 2118.

WAR DIARY
or
INTELLIGENCE SUMMARY.
(Erase heading not required.)

Instructions regarding War Diaries and Intelligence Summaries are contained in F. S. Regs., Part II. and the Staff Manual respectively. Title pages will be prepared in manuscript.

Place	Date	Hour	Summary of Events and Information	Remarks and references to Appendices
HUZECOURT	1.12.18		Ceremonial Parade. March Past. Address by Corps Cdr. Billets.	
	2.12.18		Church Parade 1030hrs.	
	3.12.18		Training in billets (wet)	
	4.12.18		Bn. Route March to AUXI-LE-CHATEAU	
	5.12.18		Specialist Training	
	6.12.18		Coy Schemes - Advance Guards, attack by locality, advance	
		0930	Billeting party sent to new area (Ailly)	
AILLY-LE-HAUT-CLOCHER	7.12.18		March to billets in AILLY-LE-HAUT-CLOCHER. Arrived 14.30 Appendix I	
AILLY-CLOCHER 8.12.18			Billets re-organised & men rested	
ABBEVILLE 9.12.18			Interior Economy & "settling in"	
	10.12.18		Bn. Ceremonial Parade. Salute taken by Officers Commanding Brigadier	
	11.12.18		Specialist Training	
	12.12.18		Educational Training Groups "A"	
	13.12.18		Route March to ABBEVILLE. Starting point 0900. Returned 1300.	
	14.12.18		Educational Training. Strict Recreational Training & Inspection	
	15.12.18		Church Parade. Athletics by Coy	

WAR DIARY
or
INTELLIGENCE SUMMARY.
(Erase heading not required.)

Army Form C. 2118.

Place	Date	Hour	Summary of Events and Information	Remarks and references to Appendices
	16.12.18		Baths 1 Coy. B/Scheme - 3 Coys. Reserve Training	
			Lecture on "Thinking." Rest Baths R.E. Games	
	17.12.18		Drill. Coys. NyaB. kept in Company during	
	18.12.18		Baths 1 Coy. Education Lectures Inspection	
	19.12.18		Billets by Brigade	
			Educational & Specialist Training	
	20.12.18	17.30	Bn. Rwta Match ST RIQUIER ROAD Games	
	21.12.18		Drill (except party) (The BLUE DAYS) P.T. Lecture on Agriculture? Games	
	22.12.18		Church Parade	
	23.12.18		Educational Training & Specialist Training Games	
	24.12.18		Holiday Games	
	25.12.18		Holiday Xmas Dinners	
	26.12.18		Holiday Games	
	27.12.18		Kit Inspection Baths 1 Coy	
	28.12.18		Educational Training Baths 1 Coy	
	29.12.18		Billet Inspection Baths 1 Coy.	

WAR DIARY
or
INTELLIGENCE SUMMARY.
(Erase heading not required.)

Army Form C. 2118.

Place	Date	Hour	Summary of Events and Information	Remarks and references to Appendices
	30.12.18		Education Games Conference by B.G.C. for Officers & N.C.O's on improvements in Arms & Equipment &c	
	31.12.18		Education Remainder Route March	
	2.1.19			

Cu.Og 11th/51 Bn The Suffolk Regt (cmdr)

SECRET.

Copy No........

11th SUFFOLKS ORDER NO 87.   6.12.18.

Ref.Sheets:- Lens 11.
Abbeville 14.

---

1. The Battalion will march tomorrow to AILLY LE-HAUT CLOCHER.

2. Starting point:- PROUVILLE CHURCH, Time :- 0925 hours.
Order of March:- Headquarters,"B","D","C","A",.
Dress:- Full Marching Order. Steel helmets will be carried on back of pack.
Route:- BEAUMETZ, LONGUILLERS-DOMQUEUR - GORENFLOS - ERGNIES, FAMECHON.
Usual distances and halts will be observed.
There will be a halt between 1130 and 1200 for one hour for dinner, which will be cooked on the march.
Battalion H.Q. and "B" Company will start from HUEZECOURT CHURCH at 0800.
"A" and "C" Coys will start from MONTIGNY at 0835.
"D" Company will start from GRIMONT at 0840.

3. Breakfasts:- 0630.
Sick Parade 0715 (Full marching order).

4. Cookers and Lewis Gun Limbers will march with Coys to Starting Point with the exception of "D" Company which will march in rear of "B" Company.

5. Baggage will be ready for collection as under:-
Battalion H.Q. at Q.M. Stores at 0730.
"A" and "C" Company at MONTIGNY CHURCH at 0800.
"B" Company on road.
"D" Company at GRIMONT ROAD JUNCTION at 0715.

6. Billets will be left scrupulously clean. Company Commander will inspect billets personally and render a clean billet certificate for each billet on attached pro forma.

7. ACKNOWLEDGE.

Captain and Adjutant.
11th (SERVICE) Bn.THE SUFFOLK REGT.(CAMBS).

Issued at 1930 hours.

Copy No 1 and 2 Retained.
3 - 6. Companies.
7. Battalion Headquarters.
8. Quartermaster.
9. Transport Officer.
10. M.O.
11. R.S.M.
12. 183rd Brigade.

WAR DIARY

11th (S) Bn The Suffolk Regt (Cambs)

January 1st – 31st 1919

Army Form C. 2118.

WAR DIARY
or
INTELLIGENCE SUMMARY.
(Erase heading not required.)

Instructions regarding War Diaries and Intelligence Summaries are contained in F. S. Regs., Part II. and the Staff Manual respectively. Title pages will be prepared in manuscript.

Place	Date	Hour	Summary of Events and Information	Remarks and references to Appendices
AILLY LE	1.1.19		Holiday. 1st Round Platoon Football Competition. 10 matches played	
HAUT CLOCHER	2.1.19		Education. Start of Group B (French, Book-keeping, Shorthand)	
	3.1.19		Education Gp A	
	4.1.19		Education Gp B	
	5.1.19		Billet Inspection	
	6.1.19		Education. Start of Demobilisation (2 men)	
	7.1.19		Education. Lecture by C.O. on Interior Economy (for Officers)	
	8.1.19		Education. Lecture by B.C. on Interior Economy " "	
	9.1.19		Education. Lecture by C.O on "Presentation of Colours" " "	
	10.1.19		Education	
	11.1.19		Education. Lecture by D.A.D.M.S. on "R.A.M.C. en voie" (200 men)	
	12.1.19		Inspection of Billets (C.O)	
	13.1.19		Education. 1st Lecture by B.G.C. on "Home Defence" (Officers)	
	14.1.19		Education. 1 Coy Baths	
	15.1.19		Education. 1 Coy Baths. 2nd Lecture by B.G.C. on Home Defence (Officers)	
	16.1.19		Education. 1 Coy Baths	

WAR DIARY
or
INTELLIGENCE SUMMARY.
(Erase heading not required.)

Army Form C. 2118.

Place	Date	Hour	Summary of Events and Information	Remarks and references to Appendices
	17.1.19		Transport Competition. 11th Suffolks v 1st S. Lancs tie 1st —	
	18.1.19		Education	
	19.1.19	10.50	Inspection of Billets	
	20.1.19		Practice for Batt Drill Competition. (Platoon) Education (Gp A)	
	21.1.19		8th Ceremonial Parade Practice Presentation of Colours	
	22.1.19		Presentation of Colours by Major Gen. J T Duncan CB "B 761st Div."	
	23.1.19		Practice for Platoon Competition Coy Rock ball Platoon	
	24.1.19		Batt Platoon Competition won by No 10 Platoon Education	
	25.1.19		Batt march to BUGNY L'ABBÉ & back Platoon Competition	
	26.1.19		Inspection of Billets	
	27.1.19		Education (A) Coy Baths	
	28.1.19		Education (Gp B) " "	
	29.1.19		Education Gp A " "	
	30.1.19		Education Gp B " "	
	31.1.19		Batt Route March	

G.L Park
Lt Col
Comdg 11th (S) Bn Suffolk Regt (Kindly)

Army Form C. 2118.

WAR DIARY
or
INTELLIGENCE SUMMARY.
(Erase heading not required.)

W.D. 41

War Diary

11th (S) Bn The Suffolk Regt (Cambs)

February 1919

Army Form C. 2118.

WAR DIARY
or
INTELLIGENCE SUMMARY.
(Erase heading not required.)

Instructions regarding War Diaries and Intelligence Summaries are contained in F. S. Regs., Part II. and the Staff Manual respectively. Title pages will be prepared in manuscript.

Place	Date	Hour	Summary of Events and Information	Remarks and references to Appendices
Abby le	1.2.19		Education Cp. B. Snow and severe frost render training difficult	
A. in Clochies	2.2.19		Lecture by C.O. on "Demobilization"	
	3.2.19		Military and Educational training. Lecture by Capt Finnigan "Australia"	
	4.2.19		Military and Educational training	
	5.2.19		Military and Educational training. One Coy Baths	
	6.2.19		Military Educational training. Performance of 1st Divis Concert Party	
	7.2.19		Lecture by 2/Lt McDavies on "The Peace Conference"	
	8.2.19		Military & Educational training One Coy Baths	
	9.2.19		Billet Inspection (C.O.) One Coy Baths	
			Orders for move to CALAIS Area received on 10th	
	10.2.19		Move postponed to 11/2/19 Collection of Area Stores etc	Indentor to Major
	11.2.19		Move by train from Longpré to AUDRUICQ (Sheet Hazebrouck 5a) Arrived 2.20 p.m	Appendix I
AUDRUICQ	12.2.19		Settling in Hut Camp Improvement of huts and camp generally	
	13.2.19		Guards on Ammunition Dump & Military Prison Escorts for Prisoners of War	
	14.2.19		Guards and Escorts	
	15.2.19		Guards and Escorts "D" Coy sent to BOURBOURG	

Army Form C. 2118.

WAR DIARY
or
INTELLIGENCE SUMMARY.
(Erase heading not required.)

Place	Date	Hour	Summary of Events and Information	Remarks and references to Appendices
ADRINICQ	16.2.19	1000	Batt Parade and Church Parade in Church put Inspection Camp (OC.)	Shaw McCarter
	17.2.19		Guards and Escorts. Very available man on duty	
	18.2.19		Guards and Escorts	
	19.2.19		Guards and Escorts	
	20.2.19		Guards and Escorts. Reinforcements 4 Officers, 1Off.R from 12th S.Suffolk Regt	
	21.2.19		Guards and Escorts. Off. Officers and 1914 O.R. found from 12th (S) B– ye Suffolk Regt., 2 Officers & 100 OR. sent to CALAIS for Escorts	
	22.2.19		Guards and Escorts	
	23.2.19		Guards. Batt Church Parade. CO's Inspection of Camp	
	24.2.19		Guards and Escorts	
	25.2.19		Guards and Escorts	
	26.2.19	11.30	Guards and Escorts. Reinforcements 2 Officers, 129 O.R. from 1/1st B" the Cambridgeshire Regiment	
	27.2.19		Guards & Escorts. Reinforcements 4 Officers, 196 O.R. from 2nd Bedfordshire Regt	
	28.2.19		Guards Escort. Reinforcement 2 Officers and 1430 R. from 1st B. Yorkshire R/L	

C.F. Fink Lt-Col
Cmdg 11 (S) B–Ye Suffolk Regt

SECRET.   Appendix I   Copy No.........
                11th SUFFOLK ORDER No.1.

Ref: EBBLINGHEM & HAZEBROUCK S.A.   7.4.24.

1.   The Battalion will move tomorrow to AUBRIOQ (sheet HAZEBROUCK
        S.A) by train from LONGPRE.
2.   First Line Transport will start at 0700 hours from Transport
        Lines. A Loading Party for transport consisting of 2nd Lt
        R.E.L. Maynard and 20 O.R's from C Company will move with the
        Transport.
            The Sergt Cook and 1 Cook per Coy will proceed with the
        Transport and prepare hot tea at LONGPRE station for 1700
        hours. Cooker dixies will be used for this.
3.   Battalion will move off at 0900 hours.
            Starting Point :   Q.M's Stores.
            Order of March :   C,D,Colours,H.Qrs, B and A Coy.
            Dress: Full Marching Order.
4.   Breakfast 0700 hours.
            Dinner ration will be issued after breakfast.
5.   Sick Parade 0800 hours (full marching Order.)
6.   Area Stores.   All area stores will be handed over to
        Q.M's representative at the Theatre at 0800 hours.
        Q.M. will hand over to Area Commandant, obtaining a receipt
        which will be forwarded to O.R.
        R.E.Stores and Ordnance Stores will be kept separate.
        Area Stores comprise : Lamps, Palliases, Stoves, Latrine
        Buckets, Ablution Benches, Washing Bowls, Tables, Forms,
        Chairs and Baths.
        Palliases will be emptied and straw burnt under Company
        arrangement.
7.   BLANKETS will be rolled in bundles of ten and stacked
        outside Coy and Battn H.Qrs by 0800 hours ready for
        Collection by lorries.
            BLANKETS MUST BE ROLLED AS TIGHTLY AS POSSIBLE TO
        ECONOMISE SPACE.
            Coys will provide their own loading parties.
8.   Officers Valises and mess kit required for breakfast
        or on the journey will be ready with Coy Blankets at 0800
        hours, or will be brought to Orderly Room by 0830 hours.
            Other Mess Stores will be placed on the Cookers which will
        be pulled out at 0800 hours.
9.   Canteen, Reading Room and Coffee Bar Stores will be
        outside O.R. at 0830 hours.
10.   Billets will be ready for Inspection by the C.O. at
        0830 hours.
11.   ACKNOWLEDGE.

                                                Captain & Adjutant.
                Issued at 2200 hours.   11th SUFFOLK Regt.

        Copies No.1 and 2. Retained.   3 - 6. Companies.
                    7 and 8. T.O. & Q.M. 9 - 10. H.Qrs & R.S.M.
                    11 and 12. Area Commandant and 103rd Brigade.

Army Form C. 2118.

WAR DIARY
or
INTELLIGENCE SUMMARY.
(Erase heading not required.)

War Diary

11th (S) Bn The Suffolk Regt (Cambs)

March 1919

WO 4 2

Army Form C. 2118.

WAR DIARY
or
INTELLIGENCE SUMMARY.
(Erase heading not required.)

Instructions regarding War Diaries and Intelligence Summaries are contained in F. S. Regs., Part II. and the Staff Manual respectively. Title pages will be prepared in manuscript.

Place	Date	Hour	Summary of Events and Information	Remarks and references to Appendices
AUDRUICQ	1.3.19		Guards and Escorts. Detachment of 2 Officers & 180 O.R. returns from CALAIS	
	2.3.19		Church Parade. Drums on Parade for the first time since being made up.	
	3.3.19		Guards and Escorts. Firing Party for Funeral of Father Carey S.J. C.F.	
	4.3.19		Guards and Escorts	
	5.3.19		Guards and Escorts	
	6.3.19		Guards and Escorts. Severe storm and continuance of wet weather	
	7.3.19		Guards and Escorts	
	8.3.19		Guards and Escorts	
	9.3.19		Guards. "B" Coy move to BOURBOURG to relieve "D" Coy.	
	10.3.19		Guards & Escorts	
	11.3.19		Guards & Escorts	
	12.3.19		Guards & Escorts	
	13.3.19		Guards & Escorts	
	14.3.19		Guards & Escorts	
	15.3.19		Guards & Escorts. Batt. Football Match v R.E.	

Army Form C. 2118.

WAR DIARY
or
INTELLIGENCE SUMMARY.
(Erase heading not required.)

Instructions regarding War Diaries and Intelligence Summaries are contained in F. S. Regs., Part II. and the Staff Manual respectively. Title pages will be prepared in manuscript.

Place	Date	Hour	Summary of Events and Information	Remarks and references to Appendices
AUDRUICQ	16.3.19		Guards. Batt^n Church Parade. C.O's Inspection of Camp.	
	17.3.19		Guards & Escorts. Performance by the Blue Boys at Opening of Church Army Hut	
	18.3.19		Guards and Escorts	
	19.3.19		Guards & Escorts. Four Officers sent to 4th Bn The Suffolk Regt.	
	20.3.19		Guards & Escorts	
	21.3.19		Guards and Escorts	
	22.3.19		Guards and Escorts. Football match v No 1 Transportation Store	
	23.3.19		Guards. Church Parade. C.O's Inspection of Camp	
	24.3.19		Guards and Escorts	
	25.3.19		Guards and Escorts	
	26.3.19		Guards and Escorts	
	27.3.19		"A" Coy returned from Zeneghem. Four officers joined for duty	
	28.3.19		Guards and Escorts	
	29.3.19		Guards and Escorts. Six Officers sent to 4th Suffolk Regt. Germany	
			"C" Coy move to No 22 Garrison Coy Camp and take over Guards of No 10 Ordnance Depot	
	30.3.19		Church Parade. C.O's Inspection of Camp	

WAR DIARY
or
INTELLIGENCE SUMMARY.
(Erase heading not required.)

Army Form C. 2118.

Place	Date	Hour	Summary of Events and Information	Remarks and references to Appendices
AUDRUICQ	31.3.19		Guards and Escorts. One Coy 2/16" London Regt marching from Reuxeman to Beaumarais stayed one night with this Batt"	

G.J. Tuck.
Lieut.-Col.
Comdg. 11th (S) Batt. The Suffolk Regt. (Cambs.)

11TH BATTALION,
SUFFOLK REGIMENT.
No.............
Date 31.3.19

Army Form C. 2118.

WAR DIARY
or
INTELLIGENCE SUMMARY.
(Erase heading not required.)

War Diary April 1919
11th (S) Batt. the Suffolk Regt (Cambs)

Vol. 43

Army Form C. 2118.

WAR DIARY
or
INTELLIGENCE SUMMARY.
(Erase heading not required.)

Instructions regarding War Diaries and Intelligence Summaries are contained in F. S. Regs., Part II. and the Staff Manual respectively. Title pages will be prepared in manuscript.

Place	Date	Hour	Summary of Events and Information	Remarks and references to Appendices
AUTREWEGE	1.4.19		Guards and Escorts	
	2.4.19		Guards and Escorts	
	3.4.19		Guards and Picots	
	4.4.19		Guards and Escorts. Football Match A Coy v D Coy won 2-0	
	5.4.19		Guards and Escorts. 4 Officers and 138 O.R. draft from 4th B. Bedfordshire Regt. Football match v Wagon Depot R.F.	
	6.4.19		Guards. Church Parade. Football match v Compressor Camp Battn. won 2-1.	
	7.4.19		Guards and Escorts	
	8.4.19		Guards and Escorts. Football Match C Coy v D Coy 'D' Coy won. 3 Officers sent to 53rd Battalion Bedfordshire Rgt. Germany.	
	9.4.19		Guards and Escorts	
	10.4.19		Guards	
	11.4.19		Guards	
	12.4.19		Guards. Major General F. J. Duncan, C.B., C.M.G., D.S.O. Commanding 61st Div visited the Battalion	
	13.4.19		Guards. Church Parade. Commanding Officer's inspection of Camp	

WAR DIARY
or
INTELLIGENCE SUMMARY.

Army Form C. 2118.

(Erase heading not required.)

Place	Date	Hour	Summary of Events and Information	Remarks and references to Appendices
AUDRUICQ	14.4.19		Guards	
	15.4.19		Guards	
	16.4.19		Guards	
	17.4.19		Guards	
	18.4.19		Guards. Good Friday. Battalion Church Parade.	
	19.4.19		Guards. Football Match. No 4 Platoon v No 14 Platoon won 5-1. A Coy	
			v D Coy. D Coy won 2-1.	
	20.4.19		Guards Garrison Church Parade. Football Match Battalion v No 4 Reserve Staying	
			Camp. Battalion won 5-0.	
	21.4.19		Guards.	
	22.4.19		Guards	
	23.4.19		Guards. Football Match A v D. D Coy won 2-0	
	24.4.19		Guards.	
	25.4.19		Guards	
	26.4.19		Guards. Sports Demonstration by team from CALAIS "D Coy (less 2 Platoons)	
			moved to Zeneghem.	
	27.4.19		Battn Church Parade	

Army Form C. 2118.

WAR DIARY
or
INTELLIGENCE SUMMARY.
(Erase heading not required.)

Place	Date	Hour	Summary of Events and Information	Remarks and references to Appendices
AURICQ	28.4.19		Guards. Three officers joined from 4th Battn Suffolk Regt., including two old officers of the Battalion	
	29.4.19		Guards	
	30.4.19		Guards. Nine officers joined from 4th Battn Suffolk Regt.	
			The prevalence of wet weather during the later part of this month caused considerable difficulty both as regards training and recreation	

Geo. J. Funke Lieut.-Col.
Comdg. 1/4th (T) Bn. Suffolk Regt. (Camb.)

Army Form C. 2118.

WAR DIARY
INTELLIGENCE SUMMARY.
(Erase heading not required.)

Instructions regarding War Diaries and Intelligence Summaries are contained in F. S. Regs., Part II. and the Staff Manual respectively. Title pages will be prepared in manuscript.

Place	Date	Hour	Summary of Events and Information	Remarks and references to Appendices

War Diary — May 1919.

11th (S) Batt" The S.uffolk Reg t (Cambs)

(1964) Wt. 4028/618 100m Pads 1/18. A. W. & Co. (2486).　　Army Form C348 (Pads).

MEMORANDUM.

From O.C.
11th (S) Batt. The Suffolk Regt. (Cambs.)
Date 1 JUN 1919 191

To HQ's
183 Inf Bde
CONFIDENTIAL.

Herewith War Diary for May 1919.

Please acknowledge receipt

G.L.J. Tuck
Lieut.-Col.
Comdg. 11th (S) Batt. The Suffolk Regt. (Cambs.)

11TH BATTALION, SUFFOLK REGIMENT.
No. K.148
Date 1 JUN 1919

WAR DIARY
INTELLIGENCE SUMMARY.
(Erase heading not required.)

Army Form C. 2118.

Place	Date	Hour	Summary of Events and Information	Remarks and references to Appendices
AUDRUICQ	1.5.19		Guards	
	2.5.19		Guards	For Health
	3.5.19		A Coy relieved C Coy at No 10 Ordnance Depot. "C" Coy returned to HQ Camp	
	4.5.19		Two officers arrived from 4th Bn Suffolk Regt. No Church Parade. About 140 men went to CALAIS by Special train for 2nd Meeting of CALAIS Area Mounted Sports.	
	5.5.19		Guards. Entertainment by "The Yellow Diamonds" in Y.M.C.A.	
	6.5.19		Guards. Meeting of mens Messing Committee. Entertainment by "The Bystanders" in Y.M.C.A.	
	7.5.19		Guards	
	8.5.19		Guards. Meeting of mens messing Committee	
	9.5.19		Guards	
	10.5.19		Guards	
	11.5.19		"VINDICTIVE" Anniversary. 100 men visited OSTEND by R.O.D Excursion	
	12.5.19		Baths and Disinfection of Blankets	
	13.5.19		Guards. Cricket Match Batt. v No 1 Transportation Stores Depot R.E.	

WAR DIARY
or
INTELLIGENCE SUMMARY.

(Erase heading not required.)

Army Form C. 2118.

Place	Date	Hour	Summary of Events and Information	Remarks and references to Appendices
AUDRUICQ	14.5.19		Guards. Baths	
	15.5.19		Guards	
	16.5.19		Guards	
	17.5.19		Guards.	
	18.5.19		100 men went by R.O.D Excursion to DUNKIRK. Battn Cricket match (all day) v No1 Transportation Stores R.E.	
	19.5.19		Visit of Brig. Gen M. Hornby C.M.G., D.S.O., commanding 183rd Inf Bde	
	20.5.19		Guards. Visit of Brig. Gen F.D.Logan, C.M.G., D.S.O., Base Commandant, CALAIS	
	21.5.19		Guards	
	22.5.19		Guards	
	23.5.19		Guards	
	24.5.19		Visit of Brig. Gen M. Hornby to AUDRUICQ BOURBOURG (B Coy) + ZENEGHEM (D Coy)	
	25.5.19		100 men went by excursion train to OSTEND	
	26.5.19		Advance party sent to ROUEN. (2 Off 70 O.R.)	
	27.5.19		B Coy + D Coy relieved by Corp of 200 th M.G. Battn and returned to AUDRUICQ	

Army Form C. 2118.

WAR DIARY
or
INTELLIGENCE SUMMARY.
(Erase heading not required.)

Place	Date	Hour	Summary of Events and Information	Remarks and references to Appendices
AUDRUICQ	28.5.19		"A" & "C" Coys relieved by two Companies of 200th M.G. Batt". Battalion concentrated in one Camp.	
	29.5.19		More postponed. Battalion Parade (the first since being made up)	
	30.5.19		Coy. Training. Battalion Parade with Transport. Surprise inspection by Brig. Gen. F.D. LOGAN, C.M.G., Base Cdr CALAIS. Transport Competition.	
	31.5.19		Coy. Training. Battalion Ceremonial Parade.	

F.W. Funk. Lieut.-Col.
Comdg. 11th (S) Batt. The Suffolk Regt. (Cambs.)

11TH BATTALION.
SUFFOLK REGIMENT.
31 MAY 1919

~ 61st Div
thro' O.C.
61st Divisional Units.
ROUEN.

CONFIDENTIAL.

Herewith War Diary for the month of June 1919.
Please acknowledge receipt.

[signature]

1-7-19.
Lieut. Colonel,
Cmdg. 11th (Service) Bn. The SUFFOLK Regiment.

Army Form C. 2118.

WAR DIARY
or
INTELLIGENCE SUMMARY.
(Erase heading not required.)

War Diary – June 1919

11th (S) Bn The Suffolk Regt (Cambs)

Army Form C. 2118.

WAR DIARY
or
INTELLIGENCE SUMMARY.
(Erase heading not required.)

Instructions regarding War Diaries and Intelligence Summaries are contained in F. S. Regs., Part II. and the Staff Manual respectively. Title pages will be prepared in manuscript.

Place	Date	Hour	Summary of Events and Information	Remarks and references to Appendices
AUDRUICQ	1.		Batt Church Parade.	
	2.		Coy Training. Platoon Demonstration	
	3		Coy. Training Battalion Ceremonial Parade. "C" Coy move to BOURBOURG for duty at No 23 Ordnance Depot	
	4		Practice for Platoon Competition.	
	5.		Companies select best platoons for Competition. Nos 3, 6, 16 Platoons chosen	
	6		Platoon Competition in Turnout Handling of Arms and Close Order Drill won by No 6 Platoon	
	7		Batt Ceremonial Parade. Sergts Mens Smoking Concert.	
	8.		Batt Church Parade	
	9		Batt less AOC Coys and part of Transport entrained at AUDRUICQ station for ROUEN Train left 16.30 hrs	Order As Appx I.
	10		Remainder spent in train. Arrived ROUEN at about 15.00 hrs. Reached Camp (G.R.B.D.) at about 1900 hrs	More App I.
ROUEN	11		Settling into new camp	

(49572) Wt. W2358/P560 6,000 12/17 D. D. & L. Sch 53a. Form/C2118/15

Army Form C. 2118.

WAR DIARY
or
INTELLIGENCE SUMMARY.
(Erase heading not required.)

Instructions regarding War Diaries and Intelligence Summaries are contained in F. S. Regs., Part II. and the Staff Manual respectively. Title pages will be prepared in manuscript.

Place	Date	Hour	Summary of Events and Information	Remarks and references to Appendices
Rouen	12.		Guards for 80 all ranks	
	13.		Guards	
	14.		Guards	
	15.		Battalion Church Parade in Church Army Hut	
	16.		Batt" move into No 2 Despatch Camp in relief of 3/6 B" Scottish Rifles	
	17.		A.o.C Corps and Remainder of transport arrived at 0200 hrs and reached camp at 0600 hrs. Visit of Major Gen J.F.Duncan (C.B. of 6th Dist)	
	18.		Guards. Re-opening of Regimental Canteen (Wet & Dry) & Reading Room	
	19.		Guards Performance by "Blue Boys" Batt" Concert Party	
	20.		Guards	
	21.		Guards	
	22.		Batt" Church Parade in Church Army Hut. Cricket match v Artillery Depot	
	23.		Guards. Entertainment in Y.M.C.A by Lena Ashwell "Concert Party.	
	24.		Guards. Cinema Entertainment in Y.M.C.A. Holiday for Peace terms being accepted	

WAR DIARY
or
INTELLIGENCE SUMMARY.
(Erase heading not required.)

Army Form C. 2118.

Place	Date	Hour	Summary of Events and Information	Remarks and references to Appendices
ROUEN	25		Guard. Battn. Disinfection of Blankets for one Coy.	
	26		Guard. Battn. one Coy. Death in Hospital of 2/Lt W.K. HARDING M.G.C.	
	27		Guard. Battn Cricket Match v 33rd Batt M.G.C.	
	28		Guard	
	29		Battn Church Parade in No.2 Convalescent Camp with 61st & 33rd B-M.G.C.	
	30		Guard. Lena Ashwell Concert Party.	
			Commencing on 23rd June it was possible to have one Coy struck off Duties entirely for purposes of training.	

G.J.P. [signature]
Lieut.-Col.
Comdg. 11th (S) Batt. The Suffolk Regt (Cambs.)

No. 1. Appendix I

ORDERS
by
LIEUT. COLONEL G.L.J.TUCK, C.M.G., D.S.O.
Commanding
11th (SERVICE) BATTALION THE SUFFOLK REGIMENT (CAMBS.)

The Battalion less "A" & "C" Companies & part of the Transport specified below, will move by train tomorrow the 9th inst. to ROUEN.

All those left behind will come under the command of O.C. "A" Company.

It is probable that "A" & "C" Coys. will move to ROUEN on the 16th inst.

I. LOADING

(a) STORES. (i) O.C. "B" Coy. will detail 1 Platoon as loading party to report to Q.M. at 1000 hours.

(ii) Blankets rolled in bundles of 10, and clearly marked with No. of platoon and Section will be stacked outside Q.M. Stores by 1000 hours. They will be collected by Companies at the Station and distributed in the trucks for use on the journey.

(iii) Stores from the undermentioned will be stacked outside Q.M. Stores by the times stated:-

1100 hours Companies & Headquarters.
            Pioneers.
            Tailors & Shoemakers.
            Canteen & Coffee Bar.
            Aid Post.
            Orderly Room.
            Sports Gear.

1330 hours. Cooking utensils required for dinner.
            Officers Kits.
            Drummers Packs.

1400 hours. Officers and Sergts. Mess Stores.

IT IS MOST IMPORTANT that these times should be strictly adhered to.

(b) TRANSPORT. (i) The Transport Officer will leave behind the undermentioned vehicles with their animals under Transport Sergt.
  "A" & "C" Coys. Lewis Gun Limbers.
  "A" & "C" Coys. Cookers.
  1 Water Cart.
  1 G.S. Wagon.

(ii) O.C. "D" Coy. will detail 1 Platoon as loading party for the Transport to report to the Transport Officer at 1315 hours. Transport will entrain during the afternoon.

II. ENTRAINING. (i) Lieut. G.R.Rogers will act as Battalion entraining Officer. He will report to the Adjutant at 1200 hours for instructions.

(ii) The train is due to leave at 1535 hours and to arrive at ROUEN at about 0600 hours on 10th inst.

(iii) The Battalion, less "A" & "C" Coys. and Transport will parade in the Camp Compound at 14.30 hours.

Dress:- Full Marching Order (Special attention is drawn to Battalion Order No. 141 para. 3 of 27.8.19)

COLOUR PARTY.
  Lieut W.G.Gentle M.C.
  No. 23634 C.S.M.Knights M.M.
  No. 15804 Sergt. W.D.Taylor D.C.M.
  No. 202333 Sergt. P.A.Jennings M.M.

(iv) Companies, Headquarters and T.O. will render

entraining state to the Orderly Room by 1200 hrs.

III. MEALS. (i) Q.M. will arrange for tea at AUDRUICQ Station at 1500 ~~1545~~ hours.
Transport Officer will detail the G.S.Wagon which is being left behind to report to the Q.M. at ~~1500~~ 14-30 hours to take tea down to the Station.
(ii) The unexpended portion of rations for the 9th will be carried on the man.
(iii) Q.M. will arrange for all available food containers to be filled with tea and taken on to the train.

Acknowledge.

E.W. Riches
Captain & Adjutant,
11th (Service) Bn The SUFFOLK Regiment.

1 & 2 retained.
3, 4, 5, & 6 Companies.
7 Headquarters.
8 Q.M.
9 T.O.
10 R.S.M.
11 Notice Board.
12 Off. Mess

Army Form C. 2118.

WAR DIARY
or
INTELLIGENCE SUMMARY.
(Erase heading not required.)

Vol 46

War Diary — July 1919

11th (S) Bn The Suffolk Regt (Cambs)

Army Form C. 2118.

WAR DIARY
or
INTELLIGENCE SUMMARY.
(Erase heading not required.)

Instructions regarding War Diaries and Intelligence Summaries are contained in F. S. Regs., Part II. and the Staff Manual respectively. Title pages will be prepared in manuscript.

Place	Date	Hour	Summary of Events and Information	Remarks and references to Appendices
ROUEN	1.7.19		Funeral of 2nd Lt H.K. Harding	
	2.7.19		Guards and Escorts	
	3.7.19		Guards, Escorts, Indian R.A. A.S.D. Mounted Sports	
	4.7.19		Guards & Escorts	
	5.7.19		Meeting of Quarterly Audit Board and Bn Messing Committee	
	6.7.19		Battn Church Parade. Battn took over extra Guards from 61st Bn	
			M.G.C. on the occasion of the latter Mounted Sports	
	7.7.19		Guards. The Commanding Officer proceeding on leave Major R.H. Carrolle assumed Command	
	8.7.19		Guards. Ceremonial Reyoluance by "Blue Boys" Concert Party	
	9.7.19		Guards	
	10.7.19		Guards	
	11.7.19		Guards reduced. Coy Practise for Ceremonial Parade	
	12.7.19		Battn Parade to Practise for Review	
	13.7.19		Final Battn Practise for Review. C.O. returned from leave	
	14.7.19		French Peace Celebrations. The Battn took part in Review and March. Again the I Congratulatory	
			Past of French troops, and represented the British troops in Rouen. Order	

Army Form C. 2118.

WAR DIARY
or
INTELLIGENCE SUMMARY.
(Erase heading not required.)

Instructions regarding War Diaries and Intelligence Summaries are contained in F. S. Regs., Part II. and the Staff Manual respectively. Title pages will be prepared in manuscript.

Place	Date	Hour	Summary of Events and Information	Remarks and references to Appendices
ROUEN	15.7.19		C.O. returned to leave. Advance Parties sent to ARRAS & PERONNE	
	16.7.19		Company Training	
	17.7.19		Company Training. Baths	
	18.7.19		Concert by the Blue Boys	
	19.7.19		British Peace Celebration Day. Holiday for all troops. Firework display in the evening	
	20.7.19		Batt" less "C" Coy move to ARRAS sub-area. Entrained at ROUEN at 16.30 hrs	Appendix II
DUISANS	21.7.19		Detrained at MAROEUIL at 11.30 hrs. Marched to "Y" Huttments. "C" Coy moved to PERONNE	
	22.7.19		Settling into new camp	
	23.7.19		"A" Coy took over guards in ARRAS area	
	24.7.19		"B" Coy took over guards in BETHUNE area	
	25.7.19		"D" Coy training	
	26.7.19		2 Officers and 6 O.R. mentioned in despatches	
	27.7.19		Cricket match "D" Coy v The Rest, won by the Rest.	
	28.7.19		Training and Guards	

Army Form C. 2118.

WAR DIARY
or
INTELLIGENCE SUMMARY.
(Erase heading not required.)

Place	Date	Hour	Summary of Events and Information	Remarks and references to Appendices
DUISANS	29.7.19		Training and Guards	
	30.7.19		Battⁿ moved to STUARTS Camp near ARRAS	
	31.7.19		Improvement of Camp.	
			On leaving ROUEN the Battⁿ passed out of the 59ᵗʰ Divⁿ (98ᵗʰ Inf Bde), and came under the administration of the 61ˢᵗ Divⁿ into No.1 Area, ARRAS Sub. Area, No.1 Area. "C" Coy came under the administration of PERONNE Sub. area, No.3 Area	

A. Wearsitte Major ent
Cmdg 11ᵗʰ Bⁿ (S) 15ᵗʰ The Suffolk Regt (Cambs)

11TH
BATTALION.
SUFFOLK REGIMENT.
31 JUL 1919

Appendix I.

J.10102/3.

O.C.,
   61/Divl. Units.

CEREMONIAL PARADE, ROUEN, JULY 14th. FRENCH NATIONAL FETE DAY.

     After today's ceremonial parade of French Troops, in which the 11th Bttn. Suffolk Regt. participated, General NOURRISSON, who commanded the parade, remarked very favourably on the steadiness of the 11th Bttn. Suffolk Regt. on parade. He also praised the manner in which the men handled their arms and carried out all movements.

     Will you kindly convey the above to Lt-Colonel G.L.J.TUCK, C.M.G., D.S.O., Commanding the 11th Bttn. Suffolk Regt., so that all ranks of the battalion may know that their Commanding Officer has received General NOURRISSON's congratulations.

Rouen. Base Hdqrs.
14th July, 1919.

Colonel,
A/Base Commandant.

Copy. No. 2.   Appendix II

ORDERS
by
MAJOR R.H. CARRETTE
Commanding
11th (SERVICE) BATTALION THE SUFFOLK REGIMENT (CAMBS.)

19-7-19.

The Battalion less "C" Company will move tomorrow to "Y" Hutments near DUISANS, ARRAS sub-area.

"C" Company will move on 21st inst. to PERONNE. Separate instructions will be issued for the latter move.

On arrival the Battalion will relieve the 4th Kings Liverpool Regiment. For this purpose Companies will eventually be disposed as follows:-

        H.Qs and "A" Coy.   DOUAI Sub-Area
               "B" Coy.   MONS   "   "

(A). LOADING.   "D" Coy.   ARRAS & BETHUNE Sub-Areas.

1. O.C. "A" Coy. will detail 1 N.C.O. & 6 men to report to the Q.M. at 0830 hours as loading party
O.C. "A" Coy. will also detail one Platoon under an Officer to report to the Q.M. at 1000 hours at the Gare du Nord. The O.C. this Platoon will be responsible that Blankets are are placed in the trucks as allotted to Companies. This Platoon will take haversack rations for dinner.

2.   Stores will be stacked outside the Q.M.Stores in Lorry loads as under by the times stated.

   (a) Canteen.   )
        Aid Post   )
        Pioneers   )
        Shoemakers.   )   0900 hours.
        Tailors.   )
        Barbers.   )
   (b) Concert Party   )
        Sports Gear.   )   0900 hours
   (c) H.Q.Stores   )
        Orderly Room Stores)
        Drummers Packs.   )   1030 hours
        Sergts. Mess   )
   (d) Officers Mess &)
        Henry Tent   )   1330 hours.

In addition to the above each Company will be allowed 1 Lorry load, to include blankets, Paliasses and stores. These will be stacked at the end of the Company lines within easy approach of a lorry by 0900 hours.
Blankets will be rolled in tens and clearly marked.
Companies will provide their own loading parties.
Officers kits will be stacked outside the Q.M.Stores by 1130 hours for loading on to baggage wagon.

3.   O.C. "B" Coy. will detail one Platoon under an Officer to report to the T.O. at the Station at 1330 hours as loading party for the Transport. All Transport will be at the Station at that hour ready for entraining.

(B). ENTRAINING.

1.   Lt. H.G. Avery is detailed as Battalion Entraining Officer He will report to the Adjutant at 0900 hours for instructions

2.   The Battalion will parade in full Marching Order at 1400 hours. Mess tins with covers on, will be carried slung from pack supporting straps.

                                                      (continued.)

2. (continued)

<u>No mugs etc., are to be slung outside the equipment.</u>

3.   The Colour Party will be as under :-
        Lt. W.G.Gentle, M.C.
        No.23634 C.S.M.Knights, M.M.
        One Sergt. to be detailed by "B" Coy.
        One Sergt. to be detailed by "D" Coy.
    Packs of the Colour Party will be sent down on the Company Lorry.

4.   Companies H.Qs. & T.O. will render entraining states to the Orderly Room by 1200 hours.

(C) **MISCELLANEOUS.**

1.   The unexpended portion of the day's rations will be carried on the man.

2.   The Q.M. will arrange for tea at the Station at 1600 hours. He will also arrange for all available food containers to be filled with tea for use on the journey.

3.   All portable Barrack equipment will be returned to Q.M. Stores by 1000 hours. All portable Barrack furniture will be assembled in Company dining rooms by 1200 hours.

4.   No lorries will be signed off except by the Adjutant or the Quartermaster.

5.   Lt. H.Williamson will remain behind to hand over to No.2 Despatch Camp and to collect men returning from leave Etc.

ACKNOWLEDGE,

                                  Captain & Adjutant.
                     11th (Service) Bn. The SUFFOLK Regt.

No. 1 Retained.
   2. War Diary.
   3, 4, 5, 6, Companies.
   7. H.Qs.
   8. Q.M.
   9. T.O.
 10. R.S.M.
 11. Notice Board.
 12. Officers Mess.
 13. Sergts. Mess.
 14. O.C. 61st Div. Units (for information.)

COPY

Appendix III

61st Division   No. A 7615

Lieut. Colonel G.L.J. TUCK, C.M.G., D.S.O.
Commanding 11th Bn. Suffolk Regt.

On the departure of the 11th Bn. Suffolk Regt., from the 61st Division in which it has served for 18 months, I should like all ranks to know in what esteem the Battalion has been held, not only by myself personally, but by the whole Division.

It has been a splendid Battalion; well known for its fighting qualities as also for its smartness and discipline behind the line.

There are a few of the old original Battalion now in the ranks, and Officers, N.C.Os. and men have been drafted into it from many other Regiments. The spirit, however, of those who made the good name of the 11th Battalion still lives, and thus it has maintained its fine reputation all through the trying time since the Armistice.

May the spirit still remain in the future of the Battalion whatever its lot may be.

The departure of the Battalion leaves a sad gap in the Division and I part with it with every regret.

In saying good-bye to you on behalf of the 61st Division I wish to place on record the high standard of efficiency, soldierly spirit and discipline of the Battalion and I wish you all the best of good futures.

(Signed)   F.J. Duncan,
Major General,
Commanding 61st Division

D.H.Q.
27.7.19.

Army Form C. 2118.

59th Div

WAR DIARY
or
INTELLIGENCE SUMMARY.
(Erase heading not required.)

Instructions regarding War Diaries and Intelligence Summaries are contained in F. S. Regs., Part II. and the Staff Manual respectively. Title pages will be prepared in manuscript.

War Diary – August 1919.

11th (S) Bn The Suffolk Regt (Cambs)

Place	Date	Hour	Summary of Events and Information	Remarks and references to Appendices

Army Form C. 2118.

WAR DIARY
or
INTELLIGENCE SUMMARY.
(Erase heading not required.)

Instructions regarding War Diaries and Intelligence Summaries are contained in F. S. Regs., Part II. and the Staff Manual respectively. Title pages will be prepared in manuscript.

Place	Date	Hour	Summary of Events and Information	Remarks and references to Appendices
ARRAS	1.8.19		A and "B" Coy Guards, "D" Coy Training. "C" Coy guards at PERONNE	
	2.8.19		Lt D.T. PIKE joined Batt" from 15th 13th Essex Regt	
	3.8.19		Batt" Church Parade. C.O. returned from leave	
	4.8.19		August Bank Holiday and general holiday. Cricket match v START Demobilisation Camp. Batt" won	
	5.8.19		Training continued	
	6.8.19		Joint temporary promotions of W.O's and NCO's made. Batt" Concert Party took to BAPAUME for one week	
	7.8.19		Training and guards continued	
	8.8.19		Orders issued for relief of "B" Coy by "D" Coy	
	9.8.19		Training and Guards	
	10.8.19		Batt" Church Parade. Batt" played ARRAS Sub area at Cricket. Arras Sub area won	
	11.8.19		"D" Coy relieved "B" Coy.	App I Order for relief
	12.8.19		Training and guards.	
	13.8.19		Training and guards	
	14.8.19		Training and guards	
	15.8.19		"B" Coy played "the Rest" at Cricket - The Rest won	
	16.8.19		Training and guards	
	17.8.19		Batt" Church Parade. Cricket match v Arras Sub Area. Sub Area won	
	18.8.19		"B" Coy second week training	

Army Form C. 2118.

WAR DIARY
or
INTELLIGENCE SUMMARY.
(Erase heading not required.)

Instructions regarding War Diaries and Intelligence Summaries are contained in F. S. Regs., Part II. and the Staff Manual respectively. Title pages will be prepared in manuscript.

Place	Date	Hour	Summary of Events and Information	Remarks and references to Appendices
ARRAS	1919			
	19.8.19		"Blue Boys" back with Battⁿ after tour in devastated area	
	20.8.19		Training and guards. "Blue Boys" Concert.	
	21.8.19		Cricket match. Battⁿ v No.3 Salvage District. Battⁿ won. Score Battⁿ 68 - Salvage 28. R/t. Law ("B"Coy) took 5 wickets with five successive balls for Battⁿ	
	22.8.19		Training and Guards. Fodder dump fire at MAROEUIL	
	23.8.19		C.O's inspection of "B" Coy	
	24.8.19		Battⁿ Church Parade. Cricket match Battⁿ v ARRAS Sub Area	
	25.8.19		Training and Guards	
	26.8.19		"B" Coy relieved "A" Coy	
	27.8.19		"A" Coy started training	
	28.8.19		Cricket match v No.8 Salvage District. Battⁿ lost by 15 runs	App "II" Orders for relief.
	29.8.19		Training and Guards	
	30.8.19		Training and Guards.	
	31.8.19		Battⁿ Church Parade	App. III Farewell letter from G.O.C 61st Div

G.I. Fate.
Lieut.-Col.
Comdg. 11th (S.) Batt. The Suffolk Regt. (Cambs.)

11TH BATTALION, SUFFOLK REGIMENT.
31 AUG 1919

Appendix I

Copy No. 2.

OPERATION ORDER No. 1
By
LIEUT. COLONEL C.L.J. TUCK C.M.G., D.S.O.
Commanding
11th (SERVICE) BATTALION THE SUFFOLK REGIMENT (CAMBS)

Ref. Maps sheet LENS 11
  "   "   "   HAZEBROUCK 5 a.

1. "D" Company will take over guards in the BETHUNE Sub-Area on the 11th instant, in relief of "B" Company and part of "A" Company. "D" Company headquarters will move to BARLIN on the same date into the Camp occupied by 47th Div'l Coy.
    The following Transport will be taken:-
        Company Commander's Charger
        1 Pack Pony
        Coy. Lewis Gun Limber Complete
        1 Bicycle.
2. Guards Nos. 1 - 7 inclusive on attached table "A" will be relieved by "D" Coy. All guards of the Battalion will return to STUARTS Camp on relief.
3. Moves of troops will be by Lorry in accordance with attached table "B". Detailed instructions will be given to each lorry driver by the Adjutant. Lorries will report at 08.30 hours and will be loaded up ready to start at 09.00 hours.
    No lorries will be signed off except by the Adjutant
4. On relief "B" Coy. will take over the Huts etc., and Barrack Furniture at present used by "D" Coy. Hut No. 4 will be handed over to "A" Coy.
5. During the afternoon or evening of the 11th inst., "A" Coy will relieve Guards Nos. 15 and 16. One lorry will be retained to effect this relief.
6. All parties will take rations for 12th inst.
7. The following guards, at present found partly by this Battalion will be found as follows, as arranged with HEADQUARTERS, BETHUNE SUB-AREA and with the O.C's Troops concerned.

Old Serial No.	Name and location	Nos. now required N.C.Os	Men	Total	To be found by N.C.Os	Men	Regt	Situation
8	"A" Dump, CAUBLAIN L'ABBE	2	21	23	1	14	L.B.L	Already at "A" Dump
					1	7	"	Fm "C" Dp
11	"C" Dump, BOYEFFLES		3	3	3	"		Already at "C" Dp
13	"D" Dump, GRANDSERVIN	1	9	10	1	9	"	Already at "D" Dp
14	VERQUIGNEUL	4	35	39	1	6	51 Lab.Coy	Already there
						13	63rd Lab.Coy	"
					1	8	20th Ldn.A.T.	"
					1	6	51st An. Lab Co.Dp.	O.M.R Hes-Digneul.
					1	5	47th Div Tm. Coy.	L.T.G. HERSIN

8. Acknowledge.

S.W.Ricker
Captain & Adjutant
11th (Service) Bn. The Suffolk Regt (Cambs)

Copy No. 1 Retained (2) War Diary, (3 - 6) Companies, (6) O.M. 7. T.O.
  8 A.D.O.   (9) P.M.C.   (10) R.T.R. (11) 98th Inf Bde.
  12 Arras Sub-Area (13) Bethune Sub-Area (14) 47th Div. Coy. (
  15 51st Lab. Coy. (16) 63rd Labour Coy. (17) R.T.O.Bethune
  18 R.T.O. Barlin, (19) R.T.O. St Pol. (20) O.C. O.M.R. Dump HESDIGNEUL
  21 O.C. "A" Dump CAUBLAIN L'ABBE.

11th (Service) Battalion The Suffolk Regiment (Camps)

Table of Duties

New Serial No.	Old Serial No.	Offrs	N.C.Os	Men	Total	Location	Nature of Duty	No. of posts	Remarks
1	5	1	6	39	46	HesDIGNEUL	O.i.B.Dump	5	4 @ 30 for Gas 2 @ 9 Empl'd
2	9	1	2	14	17	ST POL	Attd. R.T.O Ration Tns	1	
3	10	-	2	12	14	HERSIN (Bethune Sub-area H.Qs)	A.P.M.	1	
4	12	1	5	13	19	NETHUNE	H.T.	1	
5	13	-	1	6	7	BERLIN	Attd. R.T.O.RationsTns	1	
6	15	-	1	7	8	BERLIN	Attd. R.T.O.Ration Tn	1	Includes 1 Cook
7	16	-	1	12	13	BERLIN	Attd. R.S.C.Ration Dump	2	
8	1	-	4	22	26	SAINS-lxS-MARQUION	A.D.T.	3	4 @ 18 for Gds. 4 Employed.
9	17	-	3	18	21	51. B.M. 18 C.2. 5	Dump Guard	-	
10	2	-	2	7	9	ACHIET-LE-GRAND	MaLakOFF Dump Guard	1	
11	6	-	1	4	5	FREMICOURT	R.T.O.	1	
12	19	-	1	6	7	BAPAUME	N.A.C.Dump Guard	1	
13	4	-	1	6	7	DELNVILLE	R.E.Stores Guard	1	
14	3	-	2	12	14	MAROEUIL	Ord. Ammn. Dump Guard	2	
15	18	-	1	6	7	CROISIL	Ration Dump	1	attd. S/Sgt R.S.D
16	20	-	2	18	20	DUISANS	R.E.Dump Guard	3	15 hr Guard.
17	21	-	2	18	20	DUISANS	Area Sub-Area H.Q. No. 7 O.O.S	3	

Guards Nos 8 - 16 are liable to be changed.
Col. 2 shows Serial nos. originally allotted by ARRAS sub-area.

8-8-1919

Captain & Adjutant
11th (Service) Bn. The Suffolk Regiment (Camps)

TABLE "B"   11th (SERVICE) BATTALION THE SUFFOLK REGIMENT (CAMBS).

LORRY TABLE.

Outward Journey

Lorry No.	Guard No.	Total all Ranks	From	To.
1	2	17	B.H.Q. Stuarts Camp	St Pol (R.T.O.)
2	4	19	" " "	Bethune (R.T.O.)
3) 4)	1	46	" " "	Hesdigneul (O.M.B Dump)
5	3	14	" " "	Hersin (B.S.A. H.Q)
6.	5, 6, & 7	28	" " "	Barlin (R.T.O.)
7	Coy. H.Q.	–	" " "	Barlin (Coy. H.Q.s)
8	Coy. Stores	–	" " "	Barlin (Coy. H.Q.s)

Intermediate Journey

5	–	4 (plus) (7)(47th Div. Coy.)	Hersin (B.S.A. H.Qs)	Verquigneul (R.T.O.)
5	–	6 (plus) (7)(51st Lab. Coy.)	Hesdigneul (O.M.B. Dump)	Verquigneul (R.T.O.)
7	–	8 (L.H.L.)	Boyeffles (C. Dump)	Camblain L'Abbé ("A" Dump)

Return Journey

Lorry No.	Guard No.	Total all Ranks	From	To.
1	2	17	St Pol	B.H.Q. Stuart's Camp
2	4	18	Bethune	" " "
3) 4)	1	36	Hesdigneul	" " "
5	3	7/11	Hersin Verquigneul	" " "
6	5, 6 & 7	25	Barlin	" " "
7		12	Camblain L'Abbe ("A" Dump)	" " "
		10	Boyeffles (Dump "C")	" " "
8		10	Grandserving ("B" Dump)	" " "

Copy No. 2.   OPERATION ORDER No. 2.   Appendix II
by
LIEUT. COLONEL G.L.J. TUCK, C.M.G., D.S.O.
Commanding
11th (SERVICE) BATTALION THE SUFFOLK REGIMENT (CAMBS.)

Ref. Maps   LENS 11
            VALENCIENNES 12.

1. "B" Company will take over all Guards at present found by "A" Company, on the 25th inst. Table of Guards found by "A" Coy. attached.
2. Movement of troops will be by lorry in accordance with attached Table "B". Detailed instructions will be given to each lorry driver by the Adjutant. Lorries will report at 0830 hours and will be loaded up ready to start at 0900 hours.
3. "A" Company's Guards when relieved will be brought back to Stuart Camp by the lorry taking the relief. The N.C.O. in charge of each Guard will report to the Adjutant on return, relief complete or otherwise. No lorry will be signed off except by the Adjutant.
4. On relief "A" Company will take over the huts and barrack furniture etc., at present used by "B" Company. "B" Company will take over the huts etc., of "A" Company. Company Offices will not change.
5. Only the unconsumed portion of the days rations will be taken by "B" Company Guards.
6. In the event of lorries Nos. 4, 5, & 6 not being available the relief will be carried out by march route.
   Limbers will be detailed by the Transport Officer to carry the blankets and packs to these guards.
7. Acknowledge.

R.E. Good
Lieut. & A/Adjutant,

Date   Augt. 1919.   11th (Service) Bn. The SUFFOLK Regiment.

Copy. No1 Retained (2) War Diary (3 - 5) Companies (6) Q.M. (7) T.O. 8 P.M.C. (9) R.S.M. (10) 98th Infy.Bde. (11) Arras Sub-Area 12 O.C. X.A.G. Ammn. Dump SAINS LEZ MARQUION (13) C.C. MALAKOFF Dump (14) R.S.O. ACHIET-LE-GRAND (15) O.C. X.B.C. Ammn. Dump FREMICOURT (16) R.S.O. MAROEUIL (17) Camp Comdt. Arras Sub-Area 18 O.C. No.7 C.C.S.

TABLE "B"   LORRY TABLE.

Lorry No.	Gd. No.	Total all ranks.	From	To.
1.	8	26	B.H.Q. STUART CAMP	X.A.G. Ammn. Dump SAINS LEZ MARQUION.
2	9	23	" " "	MALAKOFF Dump.
3	10 & 11	21	" " "	2 & 7 to ACHIET-LE-GRAND 2 & 10 FREMI-COURT.
4	14	14	" " "	MAROEUIL
5	16	22	" " "	Sub-Area H.Q. DUISANS.
6	17	20	" " "	No.7 C.C.S. DUISANS.

TABLE "A"

11th (SERVICE) BATTALION THE SUFFOLK REGIMENT (CAMBS.)

TABLE of DUTIES.

New serial No.	Old serial No.	Offrs.	N.C.Os.	Men.	Total	Location.	Nature of Duty.	No. of Posts.	Remarks.
8	1	1	4	22	28	SAINS-LES-MARQUION.	K.A.G. Ammn. Dump.	3	4 & 18 for Gds.
9	17	1	3	19	23	51. B.H. 18 C. 2.5	Dump Guard.	3	4 Employed.
10	2	-	2	7	9	ACHIET-LE-GRAND.	MALAKOFF Dump Guard.	1	
11	6	-	2	10	12	FREMICOURT.	R.T.O. Ration Dump.	-	
14	3	-	2	12	14	MAROEUIL.	X.B.G. Dump Guard.	2	Attd. 31st R.S.D.
16	20	1	2	19	22	DUISANS.	Ration Dump.	3	
17	21	-	2	18	20	DUISANS.	Arras Sub-Area H.Q.		
							No. 7 G.C.S.		

Army Form C. 2118.

WAR DIARY
or
INTELLIGENCE SUMMARY.
(Erase heading not required.)

War Diary - September 1919 -
11th (S) Bn The Suffolk Regt (Cambs)

WAR DIARY
or
INTELLIGENCE SUMMARY.
(Erase heading not required.)

Army Form C. 2118.

Place	Date	Hour	Summary of Events and Information	Remarks and references to Appendices
ARRAS	1.9.19		"A" Coy commence 2nd week's training	
	2.9.19		Visit of Mrs Somerset, wife of the first Commanding Officer of the Regt	
	3.9.19		"A" Coy Baths	
	4.9.19		Cricket Match "A" Coy v The Rest. "A" Coy won	
	5.9.19		Training and Guards	
	6.9.19		"A" Coy Platoon Competition in Drill and Turnout, won by No 1 Platoon	
	7.9.19		Batt'n Church Parade. "A" Coy Lorry Trip to VIMY Ridge and LENS	
	8.9.19		"A" Coy Route March. Guards. 64 O.R. despatched for demobilisation	
	9.9.19		Relief of "D" Coy by "A" Coy in Bethune area guards	
	10.9.19		"D" Coy Training and Guards. "D" Coy Whist Drive	
	11.9.19		Training and Guards	
	12.9.19		Entertainment by travelling Cinema	
	13.9.19		Batt HQ's Whist Drive and Concert	
	14.9.19		Batt'n Church Parade	
	15.9.19		Football match "D" Coy v HQ's and Transport "D" Coy won 2-0	
	16.9.19		Football match Batt'n v STUART's Demobilization Camp. Draw 1-1	
	17.9.19		"D" Coy Whist Drive	
	18.9.19		Entertainment by the Blue Boys	
	19.9.19		Training and Guards	
	20.9.19		Training and Guards. General Wyatt visited the Camp	

Army Form C. 2118.

WAR DIARY
or
INTELLIGENCE SUMMARY.
(Erase heading not required.)

Instructions regarding War Diaries and Intelligence Summaries are contained in F. S. Regs., Part II. and the Staff Manual respectively. Title pages will be prepared in manuscript.

Place	Date	Hour	Summary of Events and Information	Remarks and references to Appendices
ARRAS	21.9.19		Battn. Church Parade. "B" Co. Tony trip to VIMY RIDGE & LENS.	
	22.9.19		"D" Co. Route march and Guards.	
	23.9.19		1 N.C.O. & 7 P.tes detached for demobilization.	
	24.9.19		½ "C" Coy. returned from PERONNE.	
	25.9.19		Remainder of "C" Coy. arrived from PERONNE. Football match Coy. v. The Rest. Result. The Rest won 5-0.	
	26.9.19		"B" Co. 4th Kings Liverpool arrived from DOUAI. Football match Officers v. Sergeants. Result. The Rest won 7-1.	
	27.9.19		"B" Co. Guards returned from FREMICOURT & ACHIET-LE-GRAND.	
	28.9.19		Battn. Church Parade.	
	29.9.19		"C" Coy. training. Football match Officers v. Sergeants. Officers won 2-0. "B" Co. beat "C" Co. at football 3-1.	
	30.9.19		Battn. Parade. Training.	

R.V. Vincent
Lieut-Col.
11th (S) Batt. The Suffolk Regt. (Cambs.)

G.J. Funk
Lieut (S) Batt. The Suffolk Regt. (Cambs.)

WAR DIARY

INTELLIGENCE SUMMARY

Army Form C. 2118.

War Diary
11th (S) Bn. The Suffolk Regt. (Cambs)
October 1919.

Army Form C. 2118.

WAR DIARY
INTELLIGENCE SUMMARY.
(Erase heading not required.)

Instructions regarding War Diaries and Intelligence Summaries are contained in F. S. Regs., Part II. and the Staff Manual respectively. Title pages will be prepared in manuscript.

Place	Date	Hour	Summary of Events and Information	Remarks and references to Appendices
ARRAS	1.10.19		"C" Coy. Training. Football match Officers v Sergeants. Result Officers won 4-3.	
	2.10.19		"C" Coy. Training.	
	3.10.19		"A" & "B" Coys laying duck boards & striking tents. Gen. Wyatt. (98th Bde.) visited the Battn. & gave a farewell address to the troops.	
	4.10.19		Football match Officers v Sergeants. Officers won 3-1.	
	5.10.19		Battn. Church Parade. Pony trip to VIMY RIDGE, LENS, & DOUAI.	
	6.10.19		"D" Coy. Training. "B" Co. beat "A" Co. 1-0.	
	7.10.19		Football match Officers v Sappers & Officers N⁰. 1 District. Result 1-3.	
	8.10.19		"B" & "HQ" Co. Route March. Football match with Sappers & N⁰.1 District. Result 2-2.	
	9.10.19		Battalion Cross Country 2000 hours.	
			Training.	
	10.10.19		Inter Coy Football competition. Sir Chas. Irvine Const.	
	11.10.19		Final football competition "B" Co. beat "D" Co. 1-0.	
	12.10.19		6 Officers & 142 O.R's proceed on demobilisation. Battn. Cinema parade.	
	13.10.19		Coy training Available men in 2 Companies No. 1 & 2.	
	14.10.19		6 Officers proceed to Labourgroupes	
	15.10.19		N⁰ 2 Company Whist Drive & Concert.	
	16.10.19		6 Officers & 237 O.R's proceeded to 2/23ʳᵈ London Regt. at ETAPLES.	
	17.10.19			
	18.10.19		2 Officers & 12 O.R's proceeded on demobilisation.	
	19.10.19		Pony Ride to BETHUNE.	

Army Form C. 2118.

WAR DIARY
INTELLIGENCE SUMMARY.
(Erase heading not required.)

Instructions regarding War Diaries and Intelligence Summaries are contained in F. S. Regs., Part II. and the Staff Manual respectively. Title pages will be prepared in manuscript.

Place	Date	Hour	Summary of Events and Information	Remarks and references to Appendices
ARRAS	20.10.19			
	21.10.19		1 Officer & 52 O.Rs proceeded to ETAPLES to join 2/23rd London Regt.	
	22.10.19		—	
	23.10.19		—	
	24.10.19		Football match v. Anti-aircraft Warfare Commission. Result Wiltshires won 3-1.	
	25.10.19		Lorry trip to AMIENS	
	26.10.19		—	
	27.10.19		—	
	28.10.19		22 O.Rs proceeded to ETAPLES to join 2/23rd London Regt.	
	29.10.19		—	
	30.10.19		—	
	31.10.19		—	

G.C. Tuck Lieut.-Col.
Comdg. 11th (S) Batt. The Suffolk Regt. (Cambs.)

Army Form C. 2118.

WAR DIARY

INTELLIGENCE SUMMARY.

(Erase heading not required.)

War Diary
11th (S) Bn. the Suffolk Regt. (Cambs)
November 1919

Army Form C. 2118.

WAR DIARY

INTELLIGENCE SUMMARY.

(Erase heading not required.)

Instructions regarding War Diaries and Intelligence
Summaries are contained in F. S. Regs., Part II.
and the Staff Manual respectively. Title pages
will be prepared in manuscript.

Place	Date	Hour	Summary of Events and Information	Remarks and references to Appendices
ARRAS	1.11.19			
	2.11.19			
	3.11.19			
	4.11.19			
	5.11.19			
	6.11.19			
	7.11.19			
	8.11.19			
	9.11.19			
	10.11.19			
	11.11.19		Cadre left MARŒUIL Stn. f. BOULOGNE at 1945 hours.	
	12.11.19		Arrived BOULOGNE 0200 hours.	
	13.11.19			
	14.11.19		Embarked at BOULOGNE (PRINCESS VICTORIA) arrived DOVER 10.00 a.m. Arrived CAMBRIDGE 11.35 hours. Welcome on the platform by the Lord Lieutenant of the County, the Chancellor of the University, the Mayor, all night Sheriff &c. &c. Luncheon at the LION HOTEL performance at the Theatre in the evening.	
	15.11.19			

G.I. Frick Lieut Col
Comdg. 11th (S) Batt. The Suffolk Regt.

WMS/2962 (2)

61ST DIVISION
183RD INFY BDE

11TH BN SUFFOLK REGT.
JUN 1918-NOV 1919

FROM 34 DIV 101 BDE

2.

also detail a man to report daily to O.C. No.3.Coy Divl Train to act as guide to supply wagons.

Lieut G.S.GOUGH. will act as laison Officer between Bn.H.Qrs and Q.M.Stores and Transport.

9. Sterilising water lorries are located at following points :-

    THIENNES STATION.
      I.29.c. Central.
      I.21.a. 7.2.
    Bn Dump of S.A.A. will be located about I.3.c.

10. S.A.A. can be drawn from 5th D.A.C. (BOESEGHEM) and 74th D.A.C.(BERGUETTE.)

11. ACKNOWLEDGE.

                                       Captain & Adjutant.
                                    11th Bn The SUFFOLK Regt.

Copy No.1.   C.O.
       2.   2nd in Command.
  3 - 4.   Eble.
  5 - 8.   Coys.
      9.   61st Bn M.G.C.
    10.   Bn.H.Qrs.
    11.   T.O
    12.   Q.M.
    13.   R.S.M.
    14.   183 Brigade.

www.ingramcontent.com/pod-product-compliance
Lightning Source LLC
Chambersburg PA
CBHW081405160426

43193CB00013B/2106